WIN-WIN
RELATIONSHIPS

WIN-WIN RELATIONSHIPS

9 Strategies For Settling Personal Conflicts Without Waging War

H. NEWTON MALONY, PH.D.

BROADMAN
& HOLMAN
PUBLISHERS

Nashville, Tennessee

Published by:
Broadman & Holman Publishers
Nashville, Tennessee

Book Design: Steven Boyd

4210-95
0-8054-1095-3

Dewey Decimal Classification: 254
Subject Heading: HUMAN RELATIONS \ CHURCH
Library of Congress Card Catalog Number: 94-34802

Unless otherwise indicated, Scripture quotations are taken from the King
James Version. Quotations marked NIV are from the Holy Bible, New
International Version, copyright © 1973, 1978, 1984 by International
Bible Society; NRSV, New Revised Standard Version of the Bible,
copyright © 1989 by the Division of Christian Education of the
National Council of Churches of Christ in the United States of America,
used by permission, all rights reserved; and RSV, the Revised Standard
Version of the Bible, copyrighted 1946, 1952, © 1971, 1973.

Library of Congress Cataloging-in-Publication Data
Malony, H. Newton.
    Win-win relationships: 9 strategies for settling personal conflicts
without waging war / H. Newton Malony.
       p. cm.
    ISBN 0-8054-1095-3
       1. Conflict management—Religious aspects—Christianity.
    2. Conflict management—Religious aspects—Christianity—Case
    studies. 3. Interpersonal relations—Religious aspects—Christianity.
    4. Church controversies. 5. Pastoral counseling. I. Title.
       BV4597.53.C58M35
       1995
       254—dc20
       94-34802
       CIP

To Ivoloy Bishop,
mentor and friend
from Royal Ambassador days

▼

CONTENTS

▼

PREFACE

▼

This is a personal book. I write to myself as well as to you, the reader. I think we all have problems with conflict. Far too often we go to war! We need help. I know I do. Perhaps you do too.

Handling conflict is a complex task that can be exhausting. I also think that we Christians talk a lot about peace but tend to excuse ourselves far too easily for becoming combative. Our record is not good. We need to think more seriously about how to "put our money where our mouths are."

I have tried to write a book that will do more than put you to sleep. There are many good illustrations of conflict in everyday life, and I have tried to sprinkle the chapters with an ample dose of them. Hopefully, you will find examples which are true to your experience. I trust you will be realistic, however, in remembering how difficult some of these situations have been to resolve.

At the end of some chapters are real-life case studies. Try to solve the puzzle each case presents. My desire is that you will finish the book with the feeling that you could truly handle some of those kinds of situations if they come your way. One of my goals is to increase your skill of settling conflicts "without going to war." Case studies are ideal ways to strengthen your conflict management muscles without having to pay the price of a real fight.

Most of the cases come from my experience in working with churches. However, the types of situations that these cases present can be found in families, at work, at school, in friendships, at the marketplace—almost anywhere people come together!

I have taught "conflict management" for years. Much of what is contained within these pages comes from those classes. I have focused much of my teaching on helping Christian leaders learn how to handle the difficulties that conflict can bring—both for themselves and for others. Being a Christian does not shield any of us from these sorts of problems. Conflict seems to go with the human territory.

You may not be a leader, but don't let that worry you. Each of us has the power to influence the environment in which we live. That is leadership. You can do it, and I believe you will gain much confidence if you use the ideas found in this book. Every now and then I will ask you to put the book down and engage in some exercise. Be faithful with those tasks. You will notice that your leadership skill is increasing.

Maybe the better word for leader is helper, which is the word I have used throughout the book. We can help ourselves do better when conflict arises. And we can help each other to be better at reducing conflict and solving problems.

I am a Christian. I live my life as a psychologist. I have tried to combine those two parts of me in what I have written. I do believe that our faith holds one of the more powerful answers available for handling conflict. I have not hesitated to relate the answers of faith to my psychological analysis of conflict. I hope I have been true to the best in both worlds.

Feel free to react, respond, accept, or reject what I have written. The important thing is to reflect on the issues and come to your own conclusions.

One of the distinctive differences between this book and others on the subject is my definition of *conflict*. I distinguish "problems" from "conflicts" in a way that is different from almost all other writers in the field. In my opinion, much thinking about conflict suffers from a lack of clarity. The only difference some writers make between conflicts and problems is to contend that conflicts are simply *BIG problems.*

To say that conflicts are big problems does not help us know when we are facing a conflict, from my point of view. I make a clear distinction between the two. I define problems as "differences of opinion about ways, means, or ends." Problems exist out there in the world—*between* people. Conflict, on the other hand, exists inside the mind, apart from the world—*within* the person. I define conflicts as "desperate feelings of threats to one's self-esteem that can lead to drastic acts of self-defense." Problems are concerned with ideas; conflicts are concerned with feelings. The two are not the same. Conflicts are not *big* problems; they are completly different. People go into conflict *over* problems. Conflicts are personal, individual experiences while problems are social, interindividual experiences.

As you will see, making this distinction between problems and conflicts is the crux of my argument in this book. I hope you will find this difference helpful as you pursue some ways to handle conflict without going to war. But remember, you don't have to agree with me. The important thing is that you think about the issues and come to your own conclusions.

Reading a book like this is like going on a journey. We all return different persons after trips we have taken. My wish is that this excursion along the conflict sea will have been a good one. *Bon voyage!*

▼

CHAPTER ONE

Conflicts exist inside people, not between them

▼

Things are not always what they seem to be.
— common sense saying

Truth comes to the mind so naturally
that when we learn it for the first time,
it seems as though we did no more
than recall it in our memory.
— Fontenelle (1657–1757)

▼

The title of this chapter doesn't seem to make sense. Any one of us who has walked a baby at three o'clock in the morning knows that there is a conflict *between* the baby's crying and our need for sleep. The conflict is real. It is out there between us and the crying baby. The conflict is not in our minds; we didn't just think it up.

If the baby had only remained asleep we would not be frustrated. Our impatience is because the baby is crying. We would protest strongly if someone said, "It's all in your head; you're just 'imagining' the situation."

It feels wrong to say that conflict exists *inside* people, not *between* them. Everyday experience and common sense prove otherwise. Conflicts are real; they are not fantasies. They exist in the world, not in the mind.

Many of you could probably tell me stories to prove your point that the title of this chapter has it all backward. You would point to such international conflicts as have occurred between Iraq and Kuwait over borders, between the United States and Japan over trade, between the Zulus and the ANC over power in South Africa, between the Muslims and Hindus in India over religion, and between Britain and the European Common Market over labor policies. You could also point to the divorce rate in America and the battle between liberals and conservatives over the authority of the Bible.

If those examples didn't prove that conflict exists out in the world, not just in the mind, then you could remind me of more personal situations such as family violence, parent/teen problems, neighborhood disputes, overdrawn bank accounts, automobile accidents, domineering bosses, unjust grades in school, and disagreements at church.

I know many of those stories. Let me tell you one that I think resembles many you could tell. I also think it illustrates my theory that conflicts exist in the mind, not in the world.

Bill Worthington was the chairman of the missions committee at Southside Baptist Church. He was a well-respected, influential physician in town. Pastor Martin had proposed his name for the chairmanship because he knew that Dr. Worthington had a reputation for being a strong leader. The pastor thought that he would take the job seriously and that the other committee members would follow his leadership. He had ideas. He had been on a short-term medical mission to Brazil and had a strong interest in helping disadvantaged people.

When a letter came requesting a special offering for a new mission project in rural South Korea, the pastor passed the request on to Worthington. They discussed the letter at the next committee meeting and most members felt it was a good idea. A few days after the meeting, Dr. Worthington called the church treasurer and told him to send a $4,000 check to the Korean mission.

Since church policy stated that all checks over $500 had to be approved by the board of deacons, the treasurer called Pastor Martin and asked what should be done. The pastor told the treasurer to hold up the check. In turn, he called Dr. Worthington and explained to him why the check was being delayed until the recommendation could be brought before the deacons. Pastor Martin said he was sure the recommendation would be approved.

Dr. Worthington protested that the committee had supported the expenditure and that the Korean project was in desperate need. When the pastor said he understood the urgency of the need but that church policy prevented sending the check without board approval, Dr. Worthington became offended and accused the pastor of not respecting his authority as chairman of the missions committee. He hung up the phone in anger.

Pastor Martin did not know what to do, so he turned his attention to his many other duties. In the weeks that followed, Dr. Worthington's attendance at church became spotty. He had the vice-chairman direct the next missions committee meeting and, shortly before the committee was scheduled to meet again, called Pastor Martin and resigned his position. Shortly thereafter, he transferred his membership to another church.

I think we can agree that the conflict was over the question of whether Dr. Worthington could order the $4,000 check be written and sent to Korea without the board of deacons' approval. I think we might disagree, however, about whether the real conflict was outside or inside Dr. Worthington.

My conviction is that the church policy of requiring prior approval for all checks over $500 was not the conflict. Nor was there a conflict between this policy and the Korean mission that needed the money. Until Dr. Worthington reacted as he did, the situation was just an unfortunate, but understandable, problem. The conflict arose when Dr. Worthington became infuriated. The *problem* posed by the church check-writing policy was turned into a *conflict* by Dr. Worthington himself.

I'm convinced that this is the way conflict happens—even in international disputes. The only difference between international and personal problems is the size of the issue. People go into conflict over problems. Dr. Worthington turned a problem into a conflict. The conflict was personal, not situational. The check-writing policy posed a problem for him, but that's all it was—a problem. He didn't have to turn it into a conflict. It didn't have to happen. Yet, it did! And when it did, it was inside him, not outside. He took the situation personally. The conflict was in his personal feelings. Proverbs conveys this truth when the writer states, "Pride goeth before destruction, and an haughty spirit before a fall" (16:18).

Problems are situational. Conflicts are personal. Problems exist outside of us in the world. Conflicts exist inside of us in our minds. Problems occur whenever we deal with other people. Conflicts occur when we deal with ourselves.

The best way to put it is, "People go *into* conflict *over* problems." So, Dr. Worthington went into conflict over the church's check-writing policy just as some people go into conflict over a baby's crying at three o'clock in the morning.

The problem is not the same as the conflict. Nor is the conflict the same as the problem. Problems and conflicts are different. We confuse the two. We tend to call conflicts problems and to call problems conflicts. Thinking the two are identical is understandable, but incorrect.

More importantly, if we Christians confuse conflicts with problems we will have great difficulty in preventing war. Dr. Worthington went to war. Getting mad and leaving is war. You can defeat people either by rejecting them or by destroying them. He rejected the members of the missions committee at Southside. That was war. There was a problem over when to write the check. That was real. But he treated the problem as if it were a conflict. He had to have his way. His pride made him have to win. When the missions committee did not agree with him, he rejected the church and ran away.

Thinking we have a conflict when what we have is a problem is like thinking every barbecue is a forest fire. We will be rushing around desperately trying to stop every match from being lit. We will forget that controlled fires are necessary for life. We will run the risk of declaring every flame a holocaust. We will forget that most people follow the rules and build their fires in barbecue pits and fire rings. When real danger comes we will be exhausted and confused.

Better, we should be clear about when a situation is a problem and when it could turn into a conflict in our minds. Better, we should commit ourselves to some logical and reasonable rules for problem-solving and some steps to take when we go into conflict. My brother-in-law, who runs a sheep farm near the outback in Australia, is a good example of this difference. He joins with other farmers in volunteer efforts to clear firebreaks on each side of the road to curtail major brush fires but has small fire extinguishers inside his house for small fires he might have. He doesn't confuse brushfires with burning newspapers. Nor should we confuse problems and conflicts.

Problems

Let me propose a working definition for problems. Later, I will do the same for conflicts.

Problems are differences of opinions about the ways, the means, or the ends of dealing with real-life issues.

I believe that this definition of problems will fit every situation from the protest of Indians about the lack of services in Southern Mexico to a family argument over whether to allow a twelve-year-old daughter to get her ears pierced. I am convinced that this definition will cover each conceivable predicament that might arise between Christians, ranging all the way from dialogues about which night to hold a committee meeting, to debates about whether or not a professor believes in biblical inerrancy.

All of these examples are problems. Problems are differences of opinions, different points of view, different perceptions about what to do, different understandings of the situation, different attitudes toward the leadership, different priorities about alternatives, or different outlooks on life. These differences should be called problems, not conflicts. Problems are all based on the fact that no two persons are alike. As the saying goes, "We are like some of the people some of the time but all of the people none of the time." To be a person means to have an opinion. To have an opinion means to say how things look from one's point of view of view, to see life through one's own eyes.

And because each of us has two eyes that are ours and ours alone, there will be problems—differences of opinion. Problems are normal. They are to be expected. They are natural. Problems are not bad or evil, although we often think they are.

A well-known minister I once knew would not allow any issue to be brought up at his church board meeting that he did not already know was going to pass unanimously. I used to admire his way of doing things, but I've changed my mind. I think he was mistaken. I think he confused problems with conflicts. He failed to realize that differences of opinion are normal and healthy. He must have spent a lot of energy going around convincing every board member to vote the same way. His board meetings must have been very dull without the excitement of debate. The pastor didn't seem to realize that dialogue raises motivation and enthusiasm. Nor did he know how much better a decision can be when it is worked out in open discussion.

As you can see, I think problems are good and healthy. They should be welcomed rather than avoided. Problems are the stuff of life. Christians should encourage everyone to express his or her opinion and not be afraid to take a stand.

Randy Sanders and I wrote a book called *Speak Up: Assertiveness for Christians* in which we contested the all-too-common tendency for Christians to remain silent when they should be expressing their opinions. Christians frequently claim they are being *peacemakers,* but we concluded they were being *peacekeepers.* There is a difference between peacemaking and peacekeeping. Jesus called us to be peacemakers (Matt. 5:9), but He said nothing about peacekeeping.

In fact, I think expressing our opinions is what God intended for us to do when He created humankind in His own image. In Genesis 1:26–27 we read, "And God said, Let us make man in our image, after our likeness: and let him have dominion over the fish of the sea, and over the fowl of the air, and over the cattle, and over all the earth, and over every creeping thing that creepeth upon the earth. So God created man in his own image, in the image of God created he him; male and female created he them."

We are the apex of God's creation. God intends for us to join Him in cocreating. He expects us to do something in life. He intends for us to do more than always agree with each other; to do more than always go along with what others say. He wants us to have an opinion and express it. This is what it means to be cocreators with God.

We will not always be right. Only God is right all the time. But we will not always be wrong, either, and we can join with God in trying to make the "kingdoms of this world . . . become the kingdoms of our Lord" (Rev. 11:15). God delights in problems, in my opinion. Solving problems is the way that God's creation continues.

It helps to distinguish the different types of problems. As defined earlier, "problems are differences of opinion about *ways, means,* or *ends.* Problems can be distinguished by whether they are different methods of accomplishing a goal (ways); how much time, energy, and money is to be expended in the task (means); and what are the results we want to achieve (ends). For example, the Southside Baptist/Dr. Worthington situation was not a Means problem because there seemed to be agreement that the $4,000 should be sent to the Korean mission. It was a Ways problem over the method used to send the money.

Let's see if we can fit some other situations into this distinction between ways, means, or ends.

▼ A man complains that his wife doesn't want to spend time with him anymore. This is an Ends problem. They differ in what they want to do.

▼ The United States complains that Japan won't open its markets to American products. This is a Ways problem. They differ on how they will buy and sell goods.

▼ A car owner argues with the dealer over what is covered in the warranty. This is a Means problem. They differ on how much the customer will have to pay to get the car repaired.

▼ A son becomes hurt after his best friend fails to visit his mother in the hospital when she was in an automobile accident. This is a Ways problem. The son interprets his friend's behavior as neglect and lack of caring. The friend feels misunderstood because he had to work overtime all week long.

▼ A couple becomes agitated when they receive a "second request" postcard from the secretary of the trustees for a pledge to the building fund. This is a Means problem. The couple felt the secretary should not have embarrassed them by sending another request, but the secretary simply mailed a card to all church members who hadn't made a pledge.

▼ A group of deacons sends a letter to the pastor questioning the kinds of sermons he has been preaching. The deacons feel that they are not being fed enough Bible-based teaching. This is an Ends problem. The deacons and the preacher differ on what the sermons should be like.

Stop reading for a moment and put the book down. Think about two or three situations—either current or from the past that previously you would have described as conflicts. Try to rethink each one of them as a Ways, a Means, or an Ends problem. Remember, each of the situations started out as simply differences of opinion, alternative ways of looking at situations. When you finish, take up the book again.

 Put the book down and follow the instructions.

Now, I want to clarify the meaning of conflicts. If problems are differences of opinion, then what are conflicts? If conflicts are not just big problems, then what are they?

Conflicts

A conflict is more than an extreme difference of opinion. While people are trying to solve a problem, conflicts occur when persons become so upset that they cease being reasonable and react impulsively, defensively, and drastically. Earlier, I stated, "People go into conflict over problems." We have all seen this occur. It's like people cross a line. They suddenly change. They blow their tops, throw dishes, start crying, leave the room, push and shove, become stubborn, surrender, attack, insult, plead for mercy, force agreement, shout, or run away.

Conflicts are desperate feelings of threats to one's self-esteem that can lead to drastic acts of self-defense.

A situation at a church I know of illustrates this process. Suddenly, in a discussion over the next year's plans, one of the board members stood up and slammed his fist on the table. "You never listen to me. I've been a member of this board for nine years, and you've never paid any attention to my point of view. You did it again tonight and I've had enough of it. I'm leaving, and I'm not coming back!" With this, he shoved his chair back and stormed out of the room. That was a conflict. Better said, that board member was "in conflict."

Conflict is something that occurs at a point in time. Conflict is like crossing a line. At a certain moment a person who goes into conflict crosses the line from stress to distress. Both stress and distress are feelings. They are states of mind. They are personal reactions to problem situations.

Stress is what we all feel when we face problems. No one of us wants to experience opposition to our opinions. Even though we know that differences of opinion are normal, healthy, and to be expected, we would rather not have to face them. That is normal, too. The attitude of the pastor who would not bring an issue to his board that would not pass unanimously is understandable. We can empathize with his desire. No one likes an argument.

Differences of opinion often cause strain in relationships, even when we know they are to be expected. It is natural that we should experience frustration and stress when we have to debate and compromise our points of view. But we feel most alive when we are in the stress and strain of problem solving. Stress makes our hearts beat faster and increases our alertness. That is one of the reasons why some people have said that conflicts are good for us. Life can get pretty boring, and nothing awakens us from slumber like a good fight.

What I think people really mean is that problems, not conflicts, are good for us. We can probably agree that the energy we feel in problem solving is invigorating, but I don't think we would say that the board member who stormed out of the meeting would want to repeat that experience. He was enraged, humiliated, and desperate. He was distressed, not stressed. Distressed feelings are not good feelings. Stress may be good, but distress isn't.

Whoever said that conflict was good for us was dead wrong! Conflict can destroy relationships—not build them up. Consider the following examples and see if you don't agree.

1. The pastor's eyes focused on the wife of the man whose funeral he was conducting. He saw her grief and knew he ought to comfort her, but he couldn't. He was not sad. In fact, he was thinking, *Good riddance!* The man lying in the casket had opposed almost everything he had tried to do for the last three years. He remembered the many times he had sarcastically mused to himself, *What this church needs is a few funerals.*

Have you ever felt this way about somebody who didn't agree with you? If so, you were in conflict. Was this good for the group? Does it concern you that a pastor could have had these thoughts?

2. Lightning hit the church steeple on Friday night. The church trustees met and recommended rebuilding it. Others in the congregation wanted to cap the steeple and use the money for missions. One older member offered to pay for a neon cross to be placed on top of the steeple if, and only if, the steeple was rebuilt. He said, "Anyone with good sense should know that a church without a steeple is no church at all!" He threatened to withdraw his church pledge and go to another church if the congregation did not do what the trustees recommended.

Is it only "older" members that issue ultimatums? Have you ever seen a situation where one angry ultimatum was answered with another angry ultimatum? When this happens people really are in a predicament. Everybody goes into conflict. Is this good?

3. It was coffee time at First Church. Near the stage, some members were in earnest conversation. Among their comments were: "The time has come to do something about the pastor." "He spends all his time with those new families." "He says they are the hope of the future, but we are the backbone of the church!" "Florence and Bernie said if he preached one more sermon on church growth they were going to walk out of the service." "Maybe it's time to revive that rumor about him and the church secretary. I say we need to get rid of him before it's too late."

Have you ever heard conversations similar to these? Have you ever been involved in one? Do you know any pastor who has been fired because he didn't please some group in the congregation?

What about the decision to resurrect a rumor? Was this good for the church? Was the church stronger as a result?

4. "I don't know what's gotten into those people. We teach the Bible in every Sunday School class. But the morning worship service has become a show—the choir with those fancy robes and those hard-to-understand anthems. The night service is not any better. It's outlandish! All those guitars and those ditties they sing; they'll soon be speaking in tongues! Count me out; I'm certainly not going to support those things."

Conflict is written all over this kind of talk, and I don't think this person will be a member at that church much longer. Maybe the church will split into three cliques: those who attend Sunday School, those who attend the morning service, and those who come at night. Would that be good?

All of these are examples of people who have gone into conflict over problems. They became so threatened that they took drastic action to restore their good feelings. Is conflict good? My answer is *no*; a resounding *no*—not on your life and not in the least. Those who say conflict is good for the church don't know what they are talking about. My guess is they are talking about something else—but not conflict. Conflict hurts; it does not heal.

Conflict and distress go together; problems and stress go together. The stress of problems is common; the distress of conflict is rare—thank goodness! One way to understand the relationship between stress and distress is to think about the frequency with which we typically experience these feelings. The diagram below indicates how often an average person experiences success as well as stress and distress.

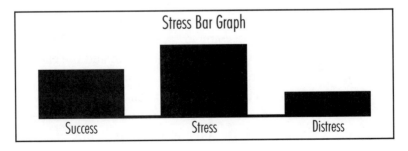

Stress Bar Graph

| Success | Stress | Distress |

Success: those times in life when our point of view carries the day, when nobody opposes what we want to do, when others give in to our opinion, when everybody cooperates with what we want to do. Success happens enough to give us fairly good self-esteem; we feel confident that most things will work out for us.

Stress: those times in life when we have to compromise, negotiate, adapt, debate, convince, accommodate, change, persuade—in other words, solve problems. Stress is the name of life's game. It is the most common of all the conditions that we face. It occurs more often than not. Like success, the strain of stress results in a positive experience enough times for us to feel fairly convinced that we can make it. We usually face problems with confidence.

Distress: those times when we go into conflict. We pass over the line from stress to desperate feelings of distress. Distress is the sense that we are in great danger of being annihilated or humiliated. These feelings are as serious as if our lives were in physical danger.

At these times, the problem pales in importance and we turn all our attention to getting rid of the distress we are feeling. On the average, these feelings of distress are rare. Usually, they occur only now and then, less often than feelings of success and far less frequently than the stress of problem solving. Distress is equal to being in conflict.

So, to sum it up, conflict is that desperate feeling of being in great danger that can lead to whatever drastic action is needed to make the situation safe for us again. The desperate feeling is the distress that if one does not do something one might be humiliated or destroyed psychologically. The drastic action that becomes possible is an effort to reduce these feelings of grave threat. Conflicts are states of mind; they are personal, inside-the-person feelings. They are not outside-the-person situations or problems. People go into conflict over problems when they feel that their opinions are not being respected, or that they will fail to persuade others, or that others might even reject them.

Problems and Conflict—Never the Twain Shall Meet

We all know this distinction between conflict and problems although we may not have thought about it in these terms. As the statement by Fontenelle at the beginning of this chapter suggests, the truth about problems and conflicts "comes to the mind so naturally." When you think about it, it makes good sense. It's good for us to reflect on our assumptions because, as the other saying put it, "Things are not always what they seem to be."

Conflict is a state of mind, not an issue of disagreement. In the examples in this chapter, the *people* were *in conflict*. In each and every case the conflict was inside the persons, not between them. The issues were not the conflict.

Facing problems may be a sign of health, not sickness. God intends for us to respect ourselves, have opinions, and solve problems. But when we become so upset and threatened that:

▼ we try to win an argument no matter who gets hurt;

▼ we think other people are so dangerous that they must be done away with;

▼ we feel we can't be seen in public and withdraw from others;

▼ we want to leave and never come back;

▼ we threaten to take our money and leave others stranded without support;

▼ we surrender to viewpoints with which we do not agree;

▼ we let people run over us and pretend we do not care;

▼ we avoid people with whom we were once friendly; . . . we are in conflict!

My guess is that every one of us can recognize ourselves in this "conflict mirror." As the well-known Australian saying puts it, "Been there, done that!"

When we identify a situation as a problem, we can calm down and endeavor to reach a reasonable solution. We can compromise or persuade. But we will not call the situation a "conflict" or become drastic in our attempts to win at any cost as long as we feel that things will work out to our advantage.

Most importantly, once we recognize this difference between conflicts and problems, we can develop our abilities to identify conflict in others, as well as ourselves, and try to reduce our distress before we do things we will regret. We can become aware of when we begin to feel desperate and try our best to stay on the problem-solving/stress side of the line without taking drastic action that we may later regret.

The case study below will give you a chance to make this distinction. It is called "December Marriage" and is about an older couple who got married in spite of the opposition of their families. Read the case, and then make a list of the primary characters. Which of them do you think is in conflict? Which of them is dealing with the stress of problem solving? What would you suggest be done?

This case study will prepare you for the next chapter, which will describe more fully what goes on inside us when we pass from the stress of problems to the distress of conflicts. It is intended to further increase your skills of self-understanding. Hopefully, this will enable you to be better able to handle conflict without waging war and thus fulfill our Lord's command to be a peacemaker.

The events in each of these case studies have really happened. They were told to me by students in my classes. I have their permission to share their experiences with you. I have changed the names and locations in an effort to protect their privacy.

▼

DECEMBER MARRIAGE

Pastor Jennings answered the telephone. It was Beatrice Smith, one of his most active parishioners.

"If you encourage my mother to marry again, I will feel like punching you in the nose!" she exclaimed with more frustration and anger than the pastor had ever heard her express before.

"All I did, Beatrice, was talk with your mother and agree with her that she did not have any scriptural reason why she could not marry," Jennings responded. "I assumed that her illness was of such a serious nature that her thoughts about marrying again were wishful fantasies. I made no definite plans with her. I don't understand your concern."

"You're right, Pastor. You don't understand. Bob and I have been taking care of Mother ever since Daddy died. We moved her next door to us and have been watching over her. If she marries Henry we will have two old people to care for. We didn't bargain for that. We won't stand idly by and let you marry them!" Beatrice shot back.

Pastor Jennings contemplated his options. Both Beatrice and her mother were long-time members of his church. He wanted to be pastor to both. He had not anticipated the distress he heard in Beatrice's voice. Although he said that her mother was probably engaging in a wishful fantasy, he had to admit she had sounded pretty serious.

Background

Several days before, Pastor Jennings was asked to call on Agnes McClanahan, the eighty-one-year-old mother of Beatrice. She was a patient in the critical care unit of a nearby hospital where she was recuperating from a hip fracture.

Soon after the pastor arrived, Mrs. McClanahan informed him that she wanted to remarry. He asked who she had in mind.

She replied, "A boy I knew in college, Henry Sidell. He is eighty-three years old now. I dated him back then and, in fact, was in love with him at one time. We each married someone else. We have both lost our mates. Now we want to get married. I'd like you to meet him. We want you to perform our wedding ceremony."

Pastor Jennings had assured Mrs. McClanahan that he would do anything he could to help her. However, he wondered if her hope of marriage was anything other than a dream. Her hip fracture was only the latest in a number of ailments that had plagued her for the past few years.

He made a date to meet Henry the next day. Henry was a well-dressed, thin, spry and alert man who was kind and attentive to Mrs. McClanahan. He asserted that he truly loved her and was more than willing to help her recuperate after she left the hospital. He spoke longingly of the possibility of their being good companions to each other in the years ahead.

Pastor Jennings assured them that he could see nothing wrong with their wishes and returned to the church to handle some administrative duties. He encouraged them to postpone making definite plans until Mrs. McClanahan was in better condition.

Several days passed. Pastor Jennings got a phone call from Mrs. McClanahan, who was still in the hospital. "I'm having some trouble with my daughter," she said. "I told them that you had said it was all right. My daughter, Beatrice, said that she couldn't envision me married to anyone except her father. When I reminded her that he had been gone for twenty years and that I was lonely, she just cried."

Pastor Jennings knew he was in for trouble. The very next day he received the call from Beatrice. In addition to threatening to punch the pastor in the nose, she said that she expected the church to support her position. She asserted that she did not want any interference from the church in her personal life and that she felt the pastor had a moral obligation not to marry her mother. She added that her son would be very upset if his grandmother loved another man like she had loved his grandfather.

Several weeks passed. Mrs. McClanahan went home from the hospital. Each day Beatrice brought Henry over to sit with her mother and have lunch with her. Although she did not want Henry to marry her mother, Beatrice saw nothing wrong with his visiting with her.

Pastor Jennings visited with Mrs. McClanahan one day. Henry was there. He tried to encourage them to think seriously about any thoughts they had of marriage and suggested that perhaps it was not the best idea.

"You don't understand me any better than my daughter does, Pastor," she said. "I want to marry Henry for companionship. I get lonely, especially at night. Beatrice and her family come over. But then they go home, and I have no one. Henry and I are in love. I want you to marry us. After all, you are my minister," she continued.

Pastor Jennings tried to intervene with Beatrice, her husband, and their son. He seemed to be getting nowhere. They were still opposed to the marriage. Then early one morning he received a call from Mrs. McClanahan. "Pastor, I wanted to tell you that we've decided to go ahead but, to ease you off the hook, we are going to have Henry's pastor perform the ceremony," she reported.

Jennings was deeply worried. Knowing what she was going to do made him an accomplice to the fact. In addition, Henry's pastor was his personal friend; Jennings knew that the pastor would be in serious trouble with the family if he performed the ceremony.

That evening Pastor Jennings heard the news. Henry's pastor had, indeed, performed the ceremony. Beatrice called him and was furious. She accused the pastor of aiding and abetting her mother. She shouted, "I can never feel the same toward you again! This is the worst thing that has ever happened to our family."

In the next few weeks, Beatrice and her family continued to attend church, sitting one or two rows from the back of the sanctuary. Beatrice always wore dark glasses as if she had been crying and did not want people to notice. They left church quickly and did not speak to anyone. Her husband began to miss deacon meetings at which he had some responsibility. Their son, with whom Pastor Jennings had always had a good relationship, became arrogant, haughty, and somewhat vindictive.

Predicament

It was Tuesday morning. Pastor Jennings sat at his desk in deep thought. The marriage of Mrs. McClanahan and Henry was an accomplished fact. Beatrice, her husband, and her son were in conflict. He empathized with their feelings. He had not meant to cause them such distress. What was he to do?

▼

CHAPTER TWO

Conflicts are a threat to self-esteem

▼

Dangers bring fears, but fears more dangers bring.
— Richard Baxter (1615–91)

Wars occur because people prepare for conflict
rather than peace.
— Trygve Lie (1896–1968)

▼

In the last chapter I stated that knowing the difference between a problem and a conflict was the first step in settling conflict without waging war. If people are not able to spot the distinction, they will not know whether they are doing conflict reduction or problem solving—two important, but different, skills.

In order to clarify this matter, we need to turn to a better understanding of what happens inside us when we go into conflict. We can't reduce conflict in ourselves or in others without a precise comprehension of what is happening when we, or they, move from the stress of problems to the distress of conflicts.

Problems—A Definition

Remember my definition of conflict: a desperate feeling that leads to drastic action. Remember, also, my definition of problems: differences of opinion about ways, means, or ends. Ends are differences of opinion over *what* is to be done. Ways are differences of opinion over *how* it is to be done. And Means are differences of opinion about the *resources* to be used in doing it. Because people tend to go into conflict *over* problems, we could say that they become distressed when they can't agree on ends, or ways, or means.

An example or two will make this clear. Suppose you have a daughter who wants to attend the senior class prom at her high school. She asks you if she can go. This is an End issue: whether or not she can go. Going or not going to the prom is the goal, or end result, of the discussion.

There may be a difference of opinion. You may not think that dancing is something a Christian girl should do. She may disagree. You debate the issue. You argue and express your different points of view. Reluctantly, you agree to let her go. The End problem is solved.

She next asks if she can go with Harvey, a young man of whom you disapprove. This is a Ways problem. She argues strongly and loudly for permission to go with Harvey. You stick to your guns. You insist that if she goes it must be with someone other than Harvey. She goes to bed crying but two days later reports that Benjamin, a boy from church, has asked her to go with him. You approve. The Ways problem of who will take her to the prom is solved, although your daughter came dangerously close to going into conflict over the outcome. Although stressed, she seemed satisfied to go with Benjamin.

Next comes the question of what she will wear. This is a Means issue. She wants a new dress that she has seen at a local shop. The two of you go shopping. The dress is far more expensive than you can afford, and you tell her no. She sulks but continues to look in other stores. After a week of shopping, you still cannot find a dress that you can afford to buy for her. Finally, she agrees to let a friend of yours make her dress. She is not happy, but begrudgingly accepts. A final problem solved: the means, or money, that will be spent to get her to the prom. On the night of the dance she looks beautiful and smiles radiantly as she leaves the house with Benjamin.

The Ways, Means, and Ends problems were solved. Everybody was *stressed* as the solutions were worked out. You and your spouse exclaim, "Whew, we're glad she's off to the dance!" as she leaves with her date. But nobody became *distressed*—not you, not your spouse, not your daughter. Nobody went into conflict: nobody allowed a desperate feeling to develop, nor did anybody behave in a drastic fashion. Arguments, yes, but hitting, no! Compromise ruled the day.

Good Faith/Bad Faith

If you want to understand the secret of problem solving, look at the assumption of good faith that underlies the process. Good faith is the key to problem solving. Good faith implies that we each know the rules of the game, that we are willing to compromise, that each of us is reasonable and fair and, most importantly, that we do not intend to ignore or destroy each other in the process.

When we doubt these basic assumptions, feel the other person is not playing by the rules, or think that the other person intends to destroy us, *bad* faith results. It is then that we go into conflict. We doubt that we can trust each other. We feel we have to defend ourselves. We act drastically, harshly, extremely, abnormally.

For most of us, however, this difference between good and bad faith is not always as neat and clear as I have described it. Speaking personally, sometimes I think I am problem solving when I am really trying to reduce the conflict in myself. At other times, I may think I am in conflict when I am not. The distinction between what is inside me, conflict, and what is outside me, problems, is often confusing and puzzling. I experience everything personally. I am easily threatened. On certain days everything seems important, and I feel very vulnerable and defensive. I flare up over the slightest disagreement and smallest affront. On other days, I am as cool as a cucumber, as the saying goes.

I wonder what the daughter or the parents in my example would say looking back on the senior prom episode? Were they ever in conflict as they decided on the ways, the means, or the ends of going to the dance? Had you been the parents, how would you answer the question?

For example, I am amazed at how upset I became recently when I made a request for a research grant, and it was turned down. If that were not embarrassing enough, when I inquired about the reasons, I learned that a good friend of mine had been asked to evaluate the proposal and had suggested that it not be approved. Later on, when I was in a meeting at which both the granting agency and my friend were present, I was asked if I still wanted the money. Bravely and nonchalantly I answered, "Well, I'm going to do some of the study anyway. If the grant comes through that will be fine; but if not, it will be all right."

When I thought back on the meeting afterward, I said to myself, "How stupid can you be? You acted like it didn't matter, just to protect your pride. It does matter! If they don't give you the money it will be because you acted like you didn't need it. You are your own worst enemy. You were in conflict and gave in when you didn't mean it." No matter how rational my behavior seemed to me at the time, I had to admit I had gone into conflict. I had gone from good faith to bad faith. I lost trust in other people and the process.

Can you identify with these examples? There is probably none of us who cannot recall similar experiences—both at home, at work, or at church. Those points at which we cease problem solving and move over into conflict are important to recognize in ourselves and to identify in others if we would settle conflict without waging war. The moment we become so distraught that we cross the line and cease to be rational is the moment we enter into conflict. The secret is our feelings. They determine the way we act in the moments that follow.

The Fine Line between Stress and Distress

This line between problems and conflict could be called the line between *stress* and *distress*. No one wants to lose an argument. All of us want to persuade others to agree with us—be it to let us have the sale item we want, to vote with us on whether to rebuild a steeple, how to worship, what pastors should do with their time, what dress our daughter should wear, or whether a project is funded. Even when compromises are reached, we want to feel that, at least, we were listened to and that some of our ideas were supported.

Every spouse has had these feelings. Every close friend can remember such experiences. Every member of a board of deacons knows what I mean. It was no fun for the deacon in the example in the first chapter to feel that "Nobody ever listens to what I have to say!"

We all are involved personally whenever we try to solve problems. Stress is involved. We want to be honored, even if we do not get our way. It is important not to be ignored or defeated.

Now, this kind of stress is good. It gives us energy and keeps us involved. All of us can recall the exhilaration we felt after an interaction in which hard problems were solved and good decisions were made. We may have been exhausted after it was over, but we were warm and satisfied inside.

What happens when we cross the line from stress to distress; from being frustrated to feeling insecure; from being upset to being in conflict? What happens is that something inside of us changes. We see things differently; we feel differently; we think differently than when we are just discussing, or debating, or arguing over some problem we are facing. We perceive the situation as getting out of hand. We think we are in grave danger. We feel exposed and threatened. We picture ourselves as about to be humiliated, even devastated. We have the sense that we might lose our place, be deeply hurt, or be in deep peril.

I've described the move from stress to distress in catastrophic terms—that may sound strange to you. I meant to exaggerate the experience in such a way that would force you to recognize that the feelings are unique. We often fail to realize when we are in conflict. We cover our feelings and dampen them by insisting that we were just trying to defend ourselves or make a point, when underneath, out of sight, inside our skins we were doing more than that. We were thinking a catastrophe was about to happen, and we were fighting for our very lives. These feelings are different in *kind*, not just *degree*, from normal feelings of tension or frustration when we are solving problems.

Consider readings on a thermometer of 99.5 and 102 degrees. We hardly notice when our body temperature increases by only one degree; but when it rises three degrees above normal, we know we are sick.

So it is with being in conflict. At first the feelings are normal—the kind of tension we experience with a slow driver in the fast lane of a freeway or when our child wants to wear old blue jeans to school on picture day. But when we argue with a merchant about the warranty on an appliance that breaks, or have to go to court with a son or daughter who is accused of spray painting cars, we can easily sense the difference in our feelings. We are close to being in conflict.

Some time ago James Rome interviewed the former Los Angeles Rams quarterback Jim Everett on an ESPN "Talk 2" television program. The interview illustrates how this change occurs. Everett, who is now with the New Orleans Saints, had a miserable time with the Rams. He was often sacked, and his passes were frequently intercepted. Sportscaster Rome had been his worst critic. In his comments, he had sarcastically taunted Everett with the name "Chris Evert"—insinuating that he played like the famous female tennis star.

Everett agreed to the television interview but asked Rome not to call him Chris Evert. In the interview, Rome ignored this request and called Jim Everett Chris once again. Everett didn't like it and asked him to stop. Rome deliberately sneered at him and said, "Chris." Everett said, "You've called me Chris for the last time." Rome responded by calling him Chris once again.

At this, Jim Everett stood up, turned over the table in front of him, and attacked Rome. He wrestled Rome to the ground and began hitting him. They had to be pulled apart. Everett crossed the line from stress to distress. He was angry and took the matter into his own hands on national television. He knew the difference between the tension he felt at the beginning of the interview and the humiliation he experienced just before he took the drastic step of attacking Rome on television—a thing he would not think of doing in his "normal" mind. The next day he said, "I don't condone the physical abuse-type thing . . . but I was put in a position that I was going to be in a journalistic-type interview and, instead, I was put into what I felt was a taunting attack."

This was a psychological event. It happened in Jim Everett's mind; it was something he felt and thought. Who is to say if he was in real danger of losing the audience's respect? Who is to say whether he had grounds for feeling that he had truly been insulted? Who is to say that the newspapers, the late-night comics, the sports writers, or the New Orleans Saints would think less of him because he had been called by a girl's name?

Of course, many of us seeing this happen would think it was unfortunate, but we might have reacted in the same manner. The situation really occurred. Rome did it right before our eyes. Calling Everett Chris Evert was insulting and uncalled for. But the catastrophe was in the mind of Jim Everett, in his interpretation of the event. And he acted out his feelings, which, like the degrees on a thermometer, were radically different from one time to another. When the degrees of his feelings went above 100, he behaved in a way that was uncivil, drastic, abnormal. Like water that had turned to steam, it felt like more a difference in *kind* than a difference in *degree*.

This is what it means to cross over from stress to distress.

Personhood and Self-Esteem

Personal involvement is the key to what goes on inside us. Our "persons" become involved whenever we try to solve problems and settle differences. Our "persons" are the people we think we are. That may sound like a funny way of putting it, but the fact remains that each of us has an opinion of ourselves that keeps us going from day to day. And whenever some difference of opinion or someone who disagrees with us comes close to endangering or threatening that self-opinion, we rise up to defend ourselves. Personhood is a "mental" event; it happens in our minds.

Someone has called this personal opinion we have of ourselves our "looking-glass self." This is to say, our self-concepts are mirror reflections of who we think others think us to be.

We play this very serious personhood game over and over and watch these signals day by day, and even moment by moment. Our antennas are always up. As long as we maintain our opinion of ourselves by more or less getting our way (either through total support or compromise), we feel OK; we can manage.

But when our opinions are ignored, when we are put down, defeated, and forced to act against our will, a signal is sent to us deep inside. Our very being is wounded; the boat is rocked; the ground underneath is shaking; our very existence is threatened;

catastrophe is upon us; our personhood is in danger. Someone has said that this sort of experience is like being put naked in the center of a ring without any clothes on where people are standing around pointing at us and either laughing at or scorning us. It's a terrible, desperate feeling. This kind of threat is what being "in conflict" is all about.

Identity and Status

Delving a bit more into this danger to our "selves," one way of thinking about ourselves is to say that we are made up of *identity* and *status*. The formula looks like this:

Identity + Status = Personhood.

Our identity is composed of all the role(s) we play in life, all the positions we hold. Status is the reputation we have as we play these roles. In both cases, we are heavily dependent on the opinions of other people. For example, students at Oxford University in England meet with their advisors each term to select tutors who will meet with them individually each week and guide their study of different topics. Should a student desire, for example, to study the history of the American Revolution, advisors will look at the list of university tutors who are specialists in that subject.

The student's advisor will choose a tutor for the student on the basis of his or her reputation or status. Many tutors are popular with the students. Others are not.

I am sure that the unpopular tutors sometimes wonder why they are not chosen, but they probably spend very little time nursing their hurt feelings because they still have their identities as "Oxford University tutors." Moreover, they probably console themselves by cherishing the free time they will have to pursue their own scholarly interests because they do not have to tutor so many students. They may experience "reputation stress"; but because their identities are secure, they do not go into conflict.

The newspapers recently reported the case of a woman who became desperate when both her identity and status were threatened. She became pregnant and could not do her work as well as before. She agreed with her employer that she should take a cut in pay, but she still retained her position. A few weeks later they fired her. She became distressed. She knew her reputation or status was compromised because she was not able to move around as easily, but she never thought her position or identity was in danger. Only when she lost them both did she go into conflict.

Take a moment to think about your personhood. What roles make up your identity? How about your status? Chart your identities by listing them on a piece of paper. These roles make up your identity.

Now, estimate your reputation in each of these roles. Is it good, fair, or poor? Put together, these ratings are your status in life.

 Put the book down and follow the instructions.

I would guess that most of your ratings were "good" or "fair" in most of the roles you play. This means that you are not under major distress at present. If you were, you would be very vulnerable to going into conflict.

In my chart of these relationships, my role as husband and father is certainly more important to me than my role as friend and teacher. However, there are times when my reputation as teacher seems to mean more to me than almost anything else. I am often puzzled why my status with students means so much to me. I get many compliments on the forms students fill out at the end of the term.

However, I remember the negative comments much longer than the positive ones. For years I have recalled the student who wrote, after a class on adult psychotherapy, "This professor needs psychotherapy!" Another student once wrote, "I have learned less in this class than in any other I have ever taken." Fortunately, I had the comfort of a loving wife who reminded me that these were exceptions.

Shifting Attention: From Outer Problems to Inner Feelings

When we have crossed the line from stress to distress we are in conflict. We no longer want to reach agreement or maintain a good relationship with others—we just want to feel better. We want to get rid of our feelings of threat, of fear, of anxiety, of anger. We are no longer problem solving; we are into conflict reduction.

A woman I know got fired from her job after she became pregnant. She sued her employer for breach of contract. She said that it was not so much the money she lost, but it was "the principle of the thing." She could just as easily have said, "I had to prove the injustice of the thing to make myself feel better."

This is the reason conflict is not good. It turns people's attention away from the problems out in the world to their inner feelings. They become preoccupied with their own feelings of distress and are so upset that they cannot make good, rational decisions. This is why conflict is not healthy. In fact, when folk are in conflict, they may subvert God's work in the world and sabotage other people's efforts to do God's will because their attention is so focused on getting rid of the feelings that are troubling them.

At this point in our discussion, somebody might ask, "Why are we so susceptible to going into conflict? to going from stress to distress?" The answer is, "Because we are human beings"—frail, weak, vulnerable human beings. Psalm 103:14 states it forthrightly: "For he knoweth our frame; he remembereth that we are dust." God says in Genesis 3:19, "Dust thou art, and unto dust shalt thou return." That is who we are; we know it, and God knows it. Going into conflict comes with the territory. Although we could live without becoming distressed, I don't know anyone who has made it all the way without going into conflict at some time. While we could live without conflict, we don't. Conflict is not necessary; it doesn't have to be. But it sure seems to be inevitable!

I suppose we all wish we could take most things in stride and realize that our self-esteem is not up for grabs as much as we might think. I recall the experience of a friend who was conducting a training workshop in Palm Springs. Time for the lunch break came, and he slipped off by himself to have lunch and prepare for what he was going to say that afternoon. After lunch he went to the restroom. As he entered the restroom he was reading his notes and did not notice that he entered the women's door instead of the men's. There were no women at the lavatories so he entered a stall without realizing he had made a mistake. A woman happened to notice his shoes and pants beneath the stall door and suspected that a man was in the room. She went outside and notified the police. They cleared the restroom and then knocked on the door to his stall.

"Yes" he answered, in what was obviously a man's voice.

No mistake had been made. It was, indeed, a man in the women's restroom.

"Are you about through?" the policeman asked.

"Just about," my friend answered. "Is there something wrong? Do you need this stall?"

"You are in the women's restroom. I gather you did not know that?"

"I certainly did *not* know that!" my friend exclaimed. "I'll be right out." Sheepishly he gathered his things together and walked out with his head down.

He told this story to a group of friends. We laughed with him and still kid him about this mistake years later. This was embarrassing but not humiliating. He took it in stride. He did not take it so personally that his self-esteem was gravely threatened. His friends laugh with him and think no less of him.

However, we fondly hope it will never happen to us. Unfortunately, it recently happened to me. I was in the Minneapolis-St. Paul airport with a lot on my mind and made the same mistake. I knew something was wrong when I heard a woman's voice outside the stall where I was sitting. I thought, at first, that it was a cleaning lady but became suspicious when I heard more than one voice and what was being said was small talk that had nothing to do with cleaning the restroom. I still didn't realize my mistake for sure until I opened the door. There was only one woman there, thank goodness. She was facing the lavatory and putting on lipstick. I hurriedly passed by her. I rushed outside and got lost in the crowd. I hope she did not see me.

Our self-esteem or personhood is the most precious possession we have, and it is so fragile that we will protect it at all costs. The distressful feelings that people have when they cross the stress/distress line are threats to self-esteem. It is our very personhoods that we feel are in great danger of being wounded, ignored, or annihilated. This is what it means to be made of dust—that material which can be blown away by the next whirlwind. We are very vulnerable to the fickle winds of fame and fortune.

Now, let's not over-spiritualize these issues too much at this point. I know that as Christians we have been encouraged to put Jesus first, others second, and ourselves third. Jesus admonished us to seek first His kingdom (Matt. 6:33). But this just isn't the way it works—most of the time. Let's admit it and acknowledge it. Nothing substitutes for good self-esteem. Nothing hurts like bad self-esteem. The desperate feeling that leads to drastic action is a self-esteem feeling, no more, no less.

I have never met a person who would not act to protect his or her self-esteem, unless that person was seriously depressed. As a psychologist, I have counseled many people about their problems and have even worked four years in mental hospitals. I have seen many people give up and act like it doesn't matter. But I know this is abnormal.

Most of us are normal in that we know the difference between stress and distress and realize that when we are in conflict it is our self-esteem that we are trying to restore. And feeling that your self-esteem is in being threatened is like having the earth move under your feet in an earthquake. Living in Southern California, I've experienced earthquakes. I have also experienced the distress of conflict. And, believe me, earthquakes and conflicts are almost the same.

Taking things personally is both a blessing and a curse. It would, of course, be best if we didn't take ourselves too seriously.

Scripture warns us not to think of ourselves more highly than we ought to think (Rom. 12:3). We are also told to love our neighbors as ourselves (Rom. 13:9). How to balance these two is the question. It seems as if, on the one hand, the Bible acknowledges that we do, indeed, love ourselves. On the other hand, we are warned not to love ourselves too much.

So, to sum it up, the second way to settle conflict without waging war is to have a clear understanding of what happens inside persons when they go into conflict. We go into conflict when we move over the line from stress to distress and do whatever it takes to restore our self-esteem. Only then is our conflict reduced to the point where we can return to solving problems. Only then can we engage in the good faith interactions that resolve our differences of opinions.

The case study that follows will give you some practice in making the distinction between a problem and a conflict. Read it through, and then ask yourself, "Is there anybody in the case who has crossed over the line from stress to distress? If so, who is it? Are either of the involved parties stressed but still in control enough to engage in problem solving? How do you know?" Answering these questions will start you along the way to mastering the skills that will help you settle conflict without waging war.

▼

I'M THE BOSS

Donald was a fresh, young seminary graduate in his first full-time ministry. He was employed as an associate of Wayne, a pastor with thirty-five years of experience who had had only one other assistant during his ministry.

At the very beginning of their time together, Wayne called Donald into his office and said, "I think it would be best that you consider me the boss. Anytime you have plans or ideas, come to me and we will discuss them. I will then decide whether or not you should pursue them. OK?"

Donald thought nothing about this arrangement because this was his first assignment and Wayne had so much more experience. However, Wayne's demand was to haunt Donald with a vengeance several months later.

One day Donald approached Wayne about working out at the local YMCA before coming to work each morning. The only problem was that this would make Donald late to work. He would arrive at the church at 8:15 rather than 8:00 A.M.

Wayne replied, "Go ahead. That's OK. I wish I could join you, but these bones are getting too old for such exercise."

So, Donald bought a membership at the Y and proceeded to work out each morning before coming to the church. He kept his agreement and arrived by 8:15 each day. Two weeks later, Wayne called Donald into his office when he arrived one morning.

Wayne stated in a matter-of-fact manner, "Donald, I think it would be best if you did not work out anymore."

"Why, Wayne, what is the problem?" Donald asked.

"You've been late from your work out, and I don't think that is fair to the church," Wayne replied.

Donald quickly reacted, "That's not fair. I was late only one day. Be reasonable. I promise I won't be late anymore."

The interchange continued: "I think you ought to quit."

"I promise I will be on time."

"No, Donald, you will not be going anymore."

"OK, what if I go from 5:00 to 6:00 in the afternoon after my office hours are over?"

"Donald, you don't have office hours. A minister is on call twenty-four hours a day."

"Oh, come on, Wayne. I know that. But nobody expects us to stay by the phone twenty-four hours and have no private life."

Finally Wayne shouted, "Donald, you are not going to work out at all. Do you understand? I'm the boss, and I am telling you what to do."

Donald shot back, "Wayne, that's not right or fair. You told me it was OK. I bought a membership at the Y. Now you tell me I can't go any time of the day. People can get me at the Y if they need me."

Wayne stared at Donald. "Didn't you hear me? The answer is no! I'm the boss."

"Well, Wayne, I guess we'll just have to settle this at the board meeting," Donald retorted as he walked out in disgust.

Predicament

Wayne was well known around the conference as a minister with great leadership skill and marked success in his past appointments. He was beginning his third year at Austinville United Methodist Church when Donald was assigned by the bishop as his assistant.

This was Donald's first full-time position, and he looked forward to the task. Donald had been a football star at a nearby church college and was well known to the youth in the area.

Although Donald was new at the church, at the next meeting of the Official Board he described his desired schedule of workouts at the YMCA and noted that Wayne had encouraged him to obtain the membership. He then went on to explain the difficulty he had with Wayne and Wayne's unreasonable request that he stop. The board then asked Wayne what he thought and he replied, "Well, I just don't think it's the best use of Donald's time." To his surprise, Donald then heard one of the board members reply, "Donald, it seems as if it would be better if you ceased your workouts." That settled the matter. The rest of the board agreed and supported Wayne.

Donald acquiesced. Over the next six months he continued to go to Wayne to share his plans and to get approval. On three occasions, Wayne approved an idea with the stipulation that he go before the board and let them know what was being planned. In each situation, when the plan was brought before the board, Wayne would say, "I don't think it's a good idea for Donald to do it." A memory of the YMCA workout episode would flash across Donald's mind.

He confronted Wayne. "Wayne, when we discussed this plan you approved of it. Now, when we come before the board, you change your mind. Wayne, that's not fair."

"Well, when I thought it over, I changed my mind," Wayne replied as if that settled the matter.

Donald continued, "You could, at least, have come to me beforehand and said that we should talk it over again before bringing it to the board. Wayne, you've done this to me again and again."

Wayne shrugged his shoulders and walked away saying, "I've got to do what I think is best for the church."

To make matters worse, every time these issues were brought up to the board, they would support Wayne by saying, "Donald, we think it best that you not do it at this time."

After the last time it happened, Donald went to the chair of the board and said, "This is not good. This is the fourth time in the past six months that I have gone to Wayne and shared my plans, and he has not supported me when we bring it to the board. I have been willing to give in because of his thirty-five years of experience. But I just cannot trust a person who tells me something is OK and then stabs me in the back at board meetings. I just cannot trust Wayne anymore. What can I do?"

The chair replied, "Donald, I know what you're going through. He did the same thing to the last youth minister."

"Is that why he left?" asked Donald.

"Yes."

"That's not right!" exclaimed Donald.

"I know it's not, but it's easier to move an assistant than it is to move a senior minister—particularly one with a track record like Wayne's. We've had some losers here, and

Wayne is like a breath of fresh air. I'll be praying for you during this trying time, Donald," the chair continued.

The next time Donald had a project he wanted to undertake he did not share anything with Wayne. At that board meeting, Donald shared his plan. As soon as he finished, someone made the motion that it be approved; it passed unanimously. Wayne was caught off guard. He said nothing. He looked bewildered.

The next morning, Wayne called Donald into his office. "Donald, what do you mean by not coming to me before you go to the board?" he questioned in a tense tone.

"Come on, Wayne, you know the answer to that. Every time I come to you, you tell me one thing. Then when we get to the board meeting you do another thing. You have stabbed me in the back too many times. I just cannot trust you at all. So, I decided to take my plan straight to the board and bypass you," Donald replied.

"But, I'm the boss!" Wayne shouted.

"Wayne, I do not agree that you're the boss when you do things like this. From now, on I am going to act as if I cannot trust you. I won't come to you. I can't afford to. It's too frustrating and distressing to me," Donald shouted and walked out of the office.

Wayne sat at his desk, dumbfounded. He could not believe what he had just heard from his assistant. He thought back on his thirty-five years of ministry. No one had ever talked like that to him before.

▼

CHAPTER THREE

Conflicts come in many colors

▼

It takes two to tango.

It takes two to *tangle* (or does it?).

It's not as much *what* happens to you,
as it is *how* you react to it.

— somewhat popular sayings

▼

Country line-dancing is the rage nowadays! In part, it is popular because you don't need a partner; you can do it alone. Not so tango-ing. You can't tango without a partner. Every tango contest I've ever seen on television showed *couples* twisting, turning, bowing, and sweeping across the floor in splendid coordination.

In a sense, conflict is more like tango-ing than country line-dancing: you can't do it alone. It takes two to *tangle*, just as it takes two to *tango*.

The July 1994 Associated Press story about a man in Riverside, California, who decided to fill his plastic wading pool with water is a perfect example. He bought the wading pool so his four children could get cool in the summer heat. As he prepared to fill the pool, a neighbor decided to mow his lawn and noticed what was happening. He claimed that the wading pool crossed the invisible property line that separated their yards.

The children's father moved the pool back a bit so the neighbor would cease complaining. However, when he wasn't looking, his wife moved the pool back to the original spot that the neighbor contended crossed his property line.

The matter quickly turned from bad to worse. The two families argued heatedly. Shouts and heated accusations filled the air. The backyard wading pool, which was intended to cool off the kids, fired up the adults instead. In the midst of the dispute, the angry neighbor went into his house and came out with a gun. Pushing and shoving erupted. The gun was fired. The father of the four children was shot. He died on the way to the hospital. It took two to tangle.

But does it? Possibly you might challenge this by saying, "You have stated that conflict is an inner state of mind, not a problem out there in the world. You have said, 'People go into conflict over problems; problems are not conflicts.' How can you now say that it takes two to tangle? Aren't you contradicting yourself?"

These are very good questions, and I can see how it might look like I'm correcting myself. I do not mean to do so. Let me explain.

You may recall the diagram in the first chapter about the three conditions of life: success, stress, and distress. I suggested that most of life was lived under the stress condition. Most of the time we are having to face the fact that things do not go exactly as we planned. Murphy's Law that "if something can go wrong, it will!" is the rule, not the exception. Life is frustrating; it takes our best energy to make it. "Things" happen. If one thing doesn't happen to you, another one will. Most of our existence requires us to overcome and deal with frustration. People get in each others' way. They see things differently, as the wading pool story vividly exemplifies. Compromise, not conquest, is the name of life's game. We survive by negotiation.

We Christians need to admit that this is not only true, but the way God intended it to be. I'm inclined to think that when God blessed Adam and Eve and told them to "Be fruitful, and multiply, and replenish the earth, and subdue it" (Gen. 1:28). He implied that it was not going to be easy. God knew that frustration and stress would be involved because He made it that way. Stress is not interference with God's plan; it is God's plan. As the Apostles' Creed asserts firmly in its opening affirmation, "I believe in God, the Father Almighty, Maker of heaven and of earth." This is God's good earth, and frustration is part of His plan. Life is the way God created it to be—problems and stress are the norm, not the exceptions.

We are not to ask God to help us avoid stress or feel that we are somehow especially blessed when we experience success without frustration. Good fortune is not a sign of God's singling a specific person out for a bonanza. Even in the Sermon on the Mount where Jesus deals with the most difficult of all human acts, forgiveness, He states clearly that God "maketh his sun to rise on the evil and on the good, and sendeth rain on the just and on the unjust" (Matt. 5:45). Sunburns and floods are the name of life's game for everybody. There is no special stress-free highway which

God has provided for Christians to use, as much as some of us would like it to be that way.

Some time ago, the minister of the Embassy of Heaven Church in Salem, Oregon, was jailed for failing to show up in court on the charge that he refused to obtain an Oregon driver's license. He claimed that he, and the members of his church, were citizens of the Kingdom of Heaven, not the state of Oregon. His church issued its own drivers' licenses and registration plates. He threatened to fast until Jesus Christ released him. His wife said her husband was obeying his Master. "If he allows men to regulate him and tell him when he can be on those highways, then he is tying to serve two masters, and no one can do that," she stated.

Unfortunately, this wife and her husband are living a delusion. As appealing as their plan might seem, we must do business with the state. There is no detour around reality. As the famous reformer Martin Luther concluded, there are two kingdoms—heaven and earth—and the Lord God made them both. We should aspire to live triumphantly in both, *at the same time.* And as long as we breathe the air of this world, frustration and stress will be our lot. It is no accident that the name of the small town where the Oregon pastor lived is Sublimity. Only tiny places can have that name, and, even there, I am quite convinced that all is not peace and harmony, as the pastor discovered when he was put in jail.

Rather than praying for less stress in our lives, we should pray, as the Lord's Prayer asserts, that God will "deliver us from evil" (Matt. 6:13). And "evil" has to do with the way problems are handled, not the problems themselves. The sad outcome of the neighbors who argued over where the wading pool would be placed exemplifies "evil." Neighbors will always dispute with each other over this or that. Their disputes are not evil; in fact, if what I contend is true, differences of opinion are part of God's intention in creation. They may be hard to accept, but they are not evil. The evil God wants to help us avoid is the kind of drastic action where neighbors kill each other or where people are put in jail out of well-intentioned stupidity.

Returning to the topic of this chapter, "Conflicts come in many colors," the "evil" or "goodness" of our reaction to the stress of life is summed up in the saying, "It's not as much *what* happens to you, as it is *how* you react to it." Stress happens, but distress does not have to! That is the conclusion I want you to affirm as we look more closely at the "colors" of conflict.

Three Sources of Stress

Stress comes from three places: the physical world, our own selves, and other people. Keep in mind that although stress may be uncomfortable to experience, it is not atypical, irregular, deviant, or unnatural. It is the norm for everyone.

The Physical World

The physical world can be frustrating and can cause problems for us. This is the world of sticks and stones and bones and matter and weather and machines, in all their manifestations.

▼ I turn the corner in my bedroom and hit my knee on the bedpost;

▼ The oil pump on my son's car breaks down and the motor burns up;

▼ We couldn't get to the beach because of a wreck on the freeway;

▼ My friend's baby was born with a hole in his heart;

▼ The computer disk which contained important data was infected with a virus and became unusable;

▼ The wind changed and brush fires destroyed many homes;

▼ I forgot to water the plants and they all died;

▼ The blood test revealed that a friend had prostate cancer;

▼ It got dark before we could finish the hunt for the lost cat;

▼ The little boy broke his arm when he fell off his bicycle;

▼ A tree fell through the roof in the recent storm;

▼ She had a flat tire on the way to meet the bus;

▼ The air conditioner broke down on the hottest day of the year;

▼ An unexpected flood destroyed the store;

▼ A truck careened across the center line and hit the car when its brakes failed;

▼ I was away on business when my son graduated from high school.

These are all examples of the stress that occurs when we come up against the laws of nature. There are physical realities out there in the world with which we all have to contend. In most of the cases mentioned above there was nothing that anyone could have done to change the situation. It just happened.

To firmly impress in your mind this type of frustration, put the book down and list some examples that come to mind. Remember, they range from the everyday to the catastrophic. Also, remember that they are part of the natural world.

 Put the book down and follow the instructions.

Personal Limitations

The second source of stress in our lives comes from ourselves. We are frustrated with our personal limitations. One of the realities of living in a computer generation is that computers do not forget, but we do. Roger Penfield, the famous neurosurgeon, discovered that by stimulating certain parts of the brain, long forgotten, incidental memories came back as if they happened yesterday. He contended that the brain recorded every event that happened as if it were a tape recorder that was never turned off.

But someway, somehow, we do forget and are unable to remember many important experiences, much less the kind of small details that Penfield's probes provoked. Maybe he was right, but who wants to walk around with electrical prods sticking out of one's head. We have to live with our personal limitations. Alzheimer's disease is only an exaggeration of what we all deal with every day.

We become distracted; we don't measure up; we come in second instead of first; we make mistakes; we are ignorant about some things; we are easily frustrated when we can't do something; our best intentions are not good enough. And, even worse, these personal stresses last a lifetime!

Psychologists tell us that our general intelligence reaches its peak in the late teen years. After that, it is all downhill. Although most adults acquire special abilities and knowledge as they age, by the time they are in their forties, they are normal, at best, in measures of general intelligence. As Shakespeare concluded, by the time of old age, we deteriorate until we are, "sans teeth, sans sight, sans everything!" And our limitations frustrate us and cause us stress.

Put the book down and recall some of your personal limitations that have provoked stress in your life. Think about your background, your appearance, your mistakes, your handicaps, your faults, your foibles, your frailties.

 Put the book down and follow the instructions.

Other People

The third, and most important source of frustration, however, is other people. This does not mean that the physical world or our own weaknesses are less important. It does mean that other people can really get in our way. They frustrate us, even when we do our best to avoid physical calamities and are willing to accept our own limitations. Other people are like "flies in the ointment" or mosquitos that sting through even the best repellent. They are always there.

I teach courses in organizational management. I define an organization as "two or more people who come together to accomplish a task that no one of them could accomplish alone."

I maintain that we cannot live without organizations. In fact, I do not believe there is much that we can do in life without "organizing." Other people are necessities, not options, for almost anything we want to do.

And other people can be very, very frustrating. As the saying goes, "My work I love; it's people I hate!" The existential philosopher, Jean Paul Sartre, stated it starkly when he said, "Hell is other people." These may put the issue in words that are a bit shocking to you, but they illustrate why this chapter began with the words, "It takes two to tangle."

Think about these examples:

▼ Children arguing over how to best care for an aging father;

▼ Citizens debating the value of an auto auction in their town;

▼ A youth begging his parents to let him stay out past midnight;

▼ Bus drivers threatening to strike for higher wages;

▼ Drivers accusing each other of causing an auto accident;

▼ A baseball manager being thrown out of the game after protesting an umpire's call;

▼ A teenager crying over not being chosen as a cheerleader;

▼ Police serving notice that a complaint has been filed about a barking dog;

▼ Spouses accusing each other of unfaithfulness;

▼ Members debating the design of a church they want to build;

▼ Workers refusing to move boxes because that is not in their union contract;

▼ Company directors firing a CEO because of falling profits;

▼ A chairman declaring the motion passed when she did not allow a formal count of the vote;

▼ A politician challenging the president to a debate;

▼ A student not being admitted to the college of her choice;

▼ Heirs disagreeing on a will's terms after a loved one's death.

I have defined problems as "differences of opinion," and these illustrations are but a few of the many, many examples of the various outlooks people have that can frustrate the rest of us.

At faculty meetings in the seminary where I teach, I have never ceased to be amazed at the variety of opinions others have on almost every issue that comes before us. There is much that goes on at these meetings about which I care very little—no matter which way the vote goes. Yet, on even the simplest issue, such as the timing of final exams, it can always be predicted that some member of the faculty will want to express an opinion and enter into a discussion. I know enough not to expect that the meeting will go smoothly without differences of opinion, but it never ceases to astonish me when it happens. Needless to say, I find it very frustrating. Perhaps the only thing that prevents me from becoming distressed over these shenanigans is the knowledge that the meeting will always end at 5:00 P.M. sharp!

It Takes Two to Tangle

How does this list of the three major frustrations of life (the physical world, personal limitations, other people) help us better understand why it takes two to tangle? The answer is twofold.

First, if there were no frustrations there would be no conflict. We go into conflict over the frustrations we experience. We have an almost irresistable tendency to move from the stress of problem solving into the distress of conflict. We allow the threats to our self-esteem that come out of the frustrations of problems to cause us to consider taking extreme action to regain our self-worth.

The "two" in the "it takes two to tangle" is always us in reaction to (1) the physical world, (2) personal limitations, or (3) other people getting in our way. The "two" are us against nature, us against ourselves, or us against other people.

However, the second understanding is this: no matter what the frustration, we still have a choice. We do not have to go into conflict. We can remain conflict-free. We can be stressed without becoming distressed, no matter what the frustration.

Do you remember the preliminary hearing in the murder of O. J. Simpson's wife? The prosecutor's and defense attorney's sparring over the testimonies of witnesses illustrates dramatically the kind of stress that can occur when people see things differently. They intensely and intentionally debate. They would like to convince the court of the rightness of one point of view.

What was most interesting about those proceedings was the relative calm that characterized the court proceedings. Lawyers are masters at keeping their cool under the most stressful court proceedings. They take their differences in stride. They assume they will argue and attack each other. It is common for attorneys on both sides of a case to socialize outside the courtroom. They don't take things personally. They accept frustration and stress as the norm. Only rarely do they let stress beome distress. They are skilled at staying out of conflict. This is rare skill.

I have a friend whose daughter recently was diagnosed as having a rare form of anemia. The daughter is one of three children, all of whom are less than six years old. When the doctor told the mother, "You will have to get used to having a child with a chronic disease," she replied, "I already know how to do that. My youngest son was in the hospital eight times in his first eighteen months with asthma and diverticulitis. My husband and I walked with him in our arms many nights as he lived through lung congestion. He is not healthy yet." As this mother told me this story, I asked, "How are you going to manage? Won't you have to cancel your plans for going back to graduate school this fall?" She replied with a smile, "No, we've managed before; we'll manage again. My family can make it."

Neither my friend nor attorneys I know minimize the seriousness of the stress they have to handle. They are aware of the realness of their problems. They are not Pollyannas. Yet, they do not give in easily nor do they avoid confrontation. They recognize that neither surrender nor victory are probable in most cases. They are good problem solvers. They define their role as "the art of the possible," not "the accomplishment of the ideal." Like good basketball players, they keep their eyes on the goal. They shoot to win and do not get caught up in personal conflicts with who happens to be guarding them at the moment. They have learned to stay out of conflict. They illustrate the value of the question that appeared on many bumper stickers during the Vietnam era: "What if they declared a war and nobody came?" Neither my friend with the sick child nor trial lawyers I know make a practice of "waging war." They illustrate the power of the saying, "It's not so much what happens to you, it's only how you take it."

However, staying out of conflict is not always possible, particularly when other persons are involved. Often, we cannot control their reactions, as the story of the wading pool illustrates. Although the father moved the pool, his wife defiantly moved it back. He, in turn, began to defend his wife. Yet, who would have predicted that this neighborhood squabble would have turned into murder? By the time the gun was fired, everyone was in conflict. The stress of the moment became distress. Each person went to war and pridefully defended his or her self-esteem. An unnecessary tragedy resulted.

I would like to suggest a model for typing conflicts that could prevent such tragedies as this. It presumes that the best thing to do is to stay "conflict-free." But it also recognizes that this is very, very difficult to do. It further presumes that those who use such a typology are interested in helping prevent war for their own and for others' sakes. As the title of this chapter notes, "conflicts come in many colors." Being able to quickly recognize these hues and tints will greatly enhance the skill of conflict reduction.

The diagram on the following page was designed by Rev. Timothy J. McMutt. It compares situations in which two people are involved. However, they differ greatly in whether or not they are in conflict, and if they are in conflict, whether or not they are in conflict over each other. Study the diagram for a moment, then I will try to make these distinctions more clear to you.

In the diagram, there are two people interacting with each other in nine different types of conditions. One individual is the Helper. By helper, I mean a person who decides to "prevent war." Helpers try to get out of conflicts themselves, and helpers try to

The Colors of Conflict

Helper

	In Over	In	Out Of
Person — In Over	(black) 9 — Person In Over 9 — Helper In Over	(red) 8 — Person In Over 6 — Helper In	(green) 7 — Person In Over 3 — Helper Out Of
Person — In	(orange) 6 — Person In 8 — Helper In Over	(gray) 5 — Person In 5 — Helper In	(blue) 4 — Person In 2 — Helper Out Of
Person — Out Of	(brown) 3 — Person Out Of 7 — Helper In Over	(yellow) 2 — Person Out Of 4 — Helper In	(white) 1 — Person Out Of 1 — Helper Out Of

assist other people to do the same. The other individual is the Person with whom the Helper is interacting.

You will notice there are three main conditions for both individuals: In Over, In, and Out Of. These stand for the different types of situations in which people find themselves.

The In Over situation is one in which either individual is in conflict over some frustrating experience with the other person. When both individuals are in the In Over condition (the upper lefthand corner, the black square), they have both gone into conflict over some problem they have with each other.

The In situation is one in which an individual has become distressed, but the frustration did not involve the other person with whom he is interacting. In this case, either the Person or the Helper, or both, are in conflict over some problem they are facing; but it does not involve each other. The middle square (the gray square) illustrates a type of situation in which both are in conflict, but not with each other. The center square of the right column illustrates a type of situation in which the Helper is not in conflict but the Person is. Yet, in this case, the Person is not in conflict over something the Helper has done.

The Out Of situation is one in which either, or neither, the Helper or the Person is in conflict at all. This kind of situation is one in which an individual is in the Stress or Success condition of life. They are either not experiencing frustration or, if they are, they are managing to handle that frustration as a problem without becoming distressed. The lower righthand corner (the white square) is an example of the situation in which both the Person and the Helper are out of conflict while the center square of the bottom row is a situation in which the Person is out of conflict but the Helper is not.

Look at the chart. There are nine combinations in which each individual is paired with the other individual in an interaction. Each person is in one of these three conditions (Out of Conflict, In Conflict, In Conflict Over the Other Person). Try your skill in describing several of the combinations.

The upper triangle is the condition the other Person is in, while the lower triangle is the situation the Helper is in. The Helper is the one doing the analysis and the one who is willing to take responsibility to help in conflict reduction. This does not mean that the other Person is helpless. However, it does assume that he or she is not the one taking the active role at this moment in the relationship.

Note that the three conditions of In Over, In, and Out Of, do not assume that the Helper is a completely unbiased, calm, always -rational individual who comes from outside the situation. More often than not, Helpers are already there before someone goes into conflict. They themselves may also have gone into conflict. Helpers are those who try to take the situation in hand

and keep war from breaking out. They are committed to conflict reduction even when they personally are feeling distressed.

Ideally, the best type of interaction would be the one in the lower righthand corner (the white square), where both the Helper and the Person were "Out Of" conflict. This type of interaction is best because each person's self-esteem is secure; and, ideally, each person is in a position to work at solving the problems in a rational manner. The stress they both are experiencing is focused on the issues with which they are dealing and is not greatly threatening to their self-esteem.

Note that the number in this lower right square is "1" in both the Helper and the Person triangle, indicating that this is the simplest and easiest type of situation for good and constructive interaction between individuals. As the numbers increase, the difficulty of conflict reduction and good problem solving increases. To assess the difficulty of reducing conflict in a given situation, multiply the two numbers together. The two extreme examples are the white and black squares. The product for the white square is 1x1=1, while that of the black square is 9x9=81. This makes sense. In the white square both the Helper and the Person are "Out Of" conflict, but in the black square they are both "In" conflict "Over" each other.

These are but illustrations of how to estimate the difficulty of each type of interactive situation. This is what is meant by the title of this chapter. Conflict does, indeed, come in "many colors." Try your hand at estimating these difficulties by multiplying the numbers in several of the boxes. See if you understand the rationale behind the different products that result.

 Put the book down and follow the instructions.

Offering Help

Settling conflict without waging war means being committed to being a "Helper." Being a Helper does not mean that one will never go into conflict. That is a delusion. But being a Helper means being against war. It means holding in one's mind the fond hope that skirmishes do not have to become major battles. It means being willing to try to control oneself even in the midst of major distress. It means being sensitive to other people's travail and having a strong desire to keep relationships on the problem-solving side of the stress/distress line.

Helpers take three steps. First, they faithfully use the Colors of Conflict graph to identify the type of situation they are dealing with *before* they jump in and try to help. They clarify for themselves what is happening in themselves and in the other Person.

Second, if they discover by the use of the graph that they are In conflict, they get themselves Out Of conflict before ever trying to help the other Person. This is a critical and crucial step that must be followed with no exceptions. Getting oneself out of conflict is something Helpers do all alone.

This means that Helpers intentionally forego the use of Defensive or Conventional methods for reducing conflict. Both of these methods involve interaction with other individuals, either to fight with them or talk to them. The only exceptions are the Flight options of Defensive conflict reduction. Instead of fleeing or surrendering, Helpers know they must get their minds in a state that will eventually let them interact with the other Person in a calm, rational, and truthful manner. Fleeing or surrendering will not meet this standard.

Helpers intentionally use Transcendent methods to reduce their conflict distress. They can do this sort of reflection alone. Helpers know how important it is that they be free of distress when they turn to helping others. They do not treat getting out of conflict lightly or hurriedly. They take the time to do it well. Helpers turn to helping others only when their self-esteem is secure and when they feel free from threats to their identities and status.

Third, Helpers try to assist the other Person in coming Out Of conflict in one of two ways. On one hand, if the other Person is In conflict but not Over the Helper, Helpers offer "understanding and support." On the other hand, if the other Person is In conflict Over the Helper, Helpers offer "apology and recognition."

In the case where the Person is In conflict but not Over the Helper, Helpers listen and provide the kind of empathy that communicates complete insight into why the Person feels the way he does. This quietens the desperate feelings of loss of self-esteem. More importantly, Helpers' empathy distills the desperate feeling that one is alone. Understanding builds trust and dampens distress. When this happens, the Person and the Helper can plan together ways to further reduce the conflict and, eventually, solve the problem. Two things should not be forgotten: (1) this type of helping works because Persons do not see these kinds of Helpers as the cause of their distress, and (2) the prime goal of this type of helping is to reduce feelings of distress in order that Persons may solve their own problems. It is not a way of smothering or taking over the life of another person.

In the case where the Person is In conflict over something the Helper did or said, the method is drastically different and more problematic. Helpers in this kind of situation must not only be out of conflict themselves, but must have taken the position that helping the other Person reduce his conflict feelings is more important than convincing the Person of the rightness of the Helper's action or position. This is a most important point for Helpers to keep in mind. It basically means that Helpers back down—even when they think they are right and did nothing wrong. The principle is that "people are more important than issues—any issue." Gaining a brother, as Matthew 18:15 puts it, become the paramount aim.

Thus the steps to follow here are *apology* and *recognition*. The apology should be for what the Helper did or said that provoked the crossing of the line from stress to distress in the Person. This does not mean that the Helper takes complete responsibility for pushing the Person into conflict. It does, however, reflect the recognition that we are all dependent on the support of others and are vulnerable to the frustrations that come from other human beings.

The apology should be specific, not general. Saying "I want to apologize for whatever I did or said that upset you" will not do the trick. Such a statement communicates to the Person that Helpers do not know what they did. Helpers are not dumb; they know. It is better to say, "I want to apologize for (specific actions) that caused you such distress. I did not mean to upset or tear you down." Christian Helpers can say this with integrity because they, indeed, are remorseful for ever thinking of other persons as expendable or worthless. They can follow such a statement with, "Please forgive me."

Only when Persons feel that Helpers sincerely regret what they did and recognize how it could cause such pain will Persons reenter into relationships and entrust themselves to conflict reduction and problem solving. In this type of situation, problem solving has to be included with conflict reduction because the occasion for going into conflict was essentially related to an issue between the Person and the Helper. This is not the case in the situation discussed above where the Person was In conflict but not over some difference with the Helper.

This chapter has considered the differing colors or types of conflict and the approach that Helpers should take in assisting other Persons reduce their conflict. Although some readers may think that I have made dealing with conflict too complicated, I would invite them to remember an example of real conflict from their own experience and see if I am not correct. Conflict is, indeed, one of life's most complicated predicaments. It calls for the best thinking that we can do. We must never forget that, unlike problems that deal with reason, conflict deals with feelings. And feelings are life's most difficult experiences to bring under control.

▼

CHAPTER FOUR

Conflicts can be reduced

▼

Conflict is the gadfly of thought. It stirs us to
observation and memory. It instigates us to action.
— John Dewey

There are more ways than one to skin a cat.
— old saying

▼

I love cats. I shudder to think of anybody "skinning" them. Yet, we all know the real meaning of that old saying; nobody thinks it applies literally to our animal friends who drink our cream and purr when we stroke them. It is a figurative statement that means there is more than one way to get where we want to go.

I live five blocks from my office. I can either walk up Euclid, turn right on Green, and then left on Los Robles, or I can walk down Cordova to Oakland, turn left, and walk until I get to the campus where I teach. There are "more ways than one to skin the cat" of getting to my office. So it is with conflict reduction.

All it takes is a little thought. That is what the quote from John Dewey implies. Dewey was a well-known, early twentieth-century educator who encouraged people to think things out. According to his quote, conflicts can be like gadflies—those irritating insects that sting cows and horses. Nobody likes conflict, but conflict can spur us to thinking and can "instigate us to action," as Dewey suggests.

Conflict is, indeed, like the sting of a gadfly; we, like horses and cows, want to get rid of its pain as quickly as we can. That is why the title of this chapter is "Conflicts can be reduced." Conflict aches; conflict hurts; conflict burns; conflict stings; conflict is pure agony.

Recall what I have said repeatedly, "Conflicts and problems are different!" While we may try to solve problems, we should try to reduce conflict. Conflict is a feeling of great discomfort. It is a desperate feeling that can lead to drastic action. When we feel bad, our prime goal is to feel better. To someone looking on, it might look like we are still trying to deal with the problem. However, beneath the surface, we are trying to reduce our distress and our anxiety.

There are at least three ways to reduce these conflict feelings—to skin the cat of conflict's desperate emotions. Following

John Dewey's recommendation, let us reflect on these options in hopes that they may help us begin inventive and thoughtful ways of reducing feelings of threat to our self-esteems.

These three basic ways to reduce conflict are Defensive, Conventional, and Transcendent. Each of them works; each of them has value; each of them can be used in combination with the other two; each of them deserves our attention; each one of them makes different assumptions about what is happening in the situation. And it is these basic assumptions that dictate which actions have to be taken to reduce the pain and suffering that conflict brings.

For example, those of us who take the Defensive way assume that other people have become enemies and are intent on hurting us. If we make this assumption, then we had better get busy and fight back to protect ourselves. The rule of thumb here is, "The best defense is a good offense." Again, those of us who take the Conventional alternative assume that others didn't intend to hurt us and that there has just been a misunderstanding. We assume we can count on everyone, believing in fairness and justice. The rule of thumb here is, "We are all friends here; time to talk is what we need." Finally, those of us who take the Transcendent alternative assume that others may or may not have intended to hurt us but their motives are not the most important thing anyway. The rule of thumb here is, "Trust in the Lord with all thine heart, and lean not unto thine own understanding" (Prov. 3:6).

More about each of these later. Let's turn to a more detailed consideration of Defensive conflict reduction.

Defensive Conflict Reduction

We are all familiar with Defensive attempts to make ourselves feel better when we are conflict-distressed. Being Defensive is probably the most natural thing to do when we feel threatened.

For example, I vividly remember shouting and waving my fist at a driver who cut in front of me just as both our cars were exiting the freeway one morning. I reacted indignantly, quickly, and defensively—not realizing until we came to a stoplight at the end of the exit that the car was the same make as that driven by the president of the seminary where I teach!

I suddenly knew that I might be in real trouble. I had shown my temper and my impulsiveness to the president of the seminary. I was deeply ashamed and didn't know what I was going to do. Fortunately, the driver turned out not to be the president. However, you can bet I have become more cautious about when I shout and raise my fist on the freeway.

This incident illustrates the two poles of Defensive efforts to reduce conflict. On the one hand is the "fight" pole. This can be seen in my shouting and shaking my fist at another driver. On the other hand is the "flight" pole. This can be seen in my intent to slump down in the seat where he could not see me, apologize profusely, or quickly turn my car away and scoot up a side street before he realized who I was—if the other driver had, indeed, turned out to be the seminary president.

Both these actions are Defensive. They are based on the underlying assumption that others have ill will toward us and do not care if they hurt or destroy us. In my case, the other driver was thought not to care whether his cutting in front of me caused me to wreck my car or not. It was each man for himself. And even if it turned out to be the president, he, too, would be the offender and might fire me if he judged me as willing to insult him for driving recklessly.

Notice how quickly I changed my behavior when I thought that I might have insulted the one who signs my salary check. Either way the event went, I was Defensive. I either attacked (fight) or escaped (flight). Either way, I would feel better after it was over. I would feel righteously justified if he heard my shouts and saw my raised fist. I would feel even better if he leaned out his window and apologized, but his seeing and hearing was enough. However, if I had made the mistake of disrespecting my superior, the president, I would need to make a hasty retreat if I could or offer a quick apology in order to gain release from the shame that had been added to my anger.

So, retreats, giving-ins, apologies—all are just as Combative as are fights, shouts, and attacks. We may not have thought this to be true, but it is. Flight as well as Fight is Combative.

Defensive reactions exist along a continuum. Some of them are instinctive and impulsive. Others are planned and intentional. All have as their single intent the reduction of distress and the restoration of self-esteem. Coming out of conflict is defined as discovering and reaffirming a basis for self-esteem that one has lost or never had. Until this happens a person is so threatened that no progress can be made in interpersonal relationships or in solving the problem at hand.

Of all Defensive options, the most primitive reaction is *escaping*. When persons escape they deny, retreat, or surrender. Denial can be seen in adults who disavow that they were abused when they were children. To a lesser degree, denial can be seen in persons who assume a stoic attitude and claim that events don't affect them. When asked if they are upset they often respond, "Who, me? Not in the least!" When approached about an issue that they once felt strongly about, they sometimes respond, "I don't know why I got so upset about such a trivial matter."

People also restore their self esteem by retreating or "fleeing the scene." They think the only way they can restore their sense of self worth is to get out of the situation. This type of escape is the "flight" part of defense at its best.

On the old television program "All in the Family," Archie Bunker would sometimes get so upset that he went to the closet, put on his jacket and hat, and said, "Edith, I'm going down to the bar to get away from all this." We have all known church members who disappeared. They got angry and left rather than stay. As the old adage puts it, "Some church people vote with their feet and their pocketbook; when they get upset they leave and they quit giving."

Yet another Defensive way persons react to conflict is by *depreciating* themselves. They surrender and give in. They suddenly change their minds and agree with the opposition, even when they don't really mean it. This resembles the old admonition, "If you can't beat them, join them." The restoration of their self-esteem is made possible by the devaluing of their own ideas or opinions. We've all seen persons who give up on their points of view to receive the pity, the condescension, or the approval of others. As the old saying suggests, sometimes it feels like "It is better to be wanted for murder than not to be wanted at all."

"Fight" defenses are more familiar than "flight" defenses, however. Some of these types of reactions occur before a major affront has occurred. They are defensive reactions based on the perception that one has not yet been attacked but that one might be. Being assertive in an argument is sometimes based on the feeling that one is about to be defeated and that one's pride is threatened. How many times in a debate over how to spend the church's mission money have we seen persons suddenly straighten up out of their seats, raise their voices, and speak their minds very loudly. Often, this reaction works. People pay attention. They become convinced and persuaded.

At times, assertion can be a little more subtle but just as effective. After my friend's husband died she wanted to refurbish a piano and place it in the church sanctuary in his memory. Some folk opposed this. She started a telephone calling campaign. "Don't tell anyone I called, but I want your vote for the piano next week at the church board meeting. Horace was a faithful member of the choir, and I am sure you would want to honor him in this way." At the board meeting, the vote went her way. She would have felt very disappointed had they voted against her idea. As she said, "It was the principle of the thing, more than the piano." Her assertion worked.

Intimidation or threat is a variation on the assertion theme. My friend's implication that a vote against her piano project would be a vote to dishonor her deceased husband was a veiled threat. It was on the border between assertion and intimidation. Often, threats are not as subtle. The gorilla who growls and beats his chest is the classic example of a threat. "Stop what you are doing! Stay away from me! I will defend myself if you come one step closer! If you don't believe me, try me! Make my day!" These are the voices of intimidation. They can be heard in words, seen in looks, felt by gestures.

Aggression, however, goes a step beyond assertion. Aggression is an attack against other persons rather than just a threat. The presumption is that if one acts aggressive enough, the other person will back away and give up on the issue. Then one will win the battle, thus preserving self-esteem. It is based on the philosophy of "Hurt before being hurt." I remember the first fight I ever won. I was pretty much of a sissy. I didn't think I could defend myself, so I exerted a lot of energy staying away from a challenge or accepting defeat by crouching and taking the blows. In my senior year of high school I won my first fight. I was aggressive. A big end on the football team harassed me mercilessly in my gym class. He would throw the football at me when I was not looking and hit me in the back. As we were walking off the field one day, I suddenly had had enough of his torment. I quickly picked up the ball and threw it back at him with all my might. I will never forget the look in his eyes as I followed the ball with my fist. I have never felt defenseless again.

Sometimes aggression can be more psychological than physical, however. We all know situations in which rumors got started and persons were discounted and discredited—because of some attack on them as persons. Often, this kind of Defensive behavior is subtle. It can seem so righteous and moral to spread rumors. I remember a family who was hurt that their pastor had replaced their father as church school superintendent. After this happened they spread rumors about his preaching that eventually cost him his job.

This leads us to the type of reaction we think of most often in the Defensive way to reduce conflict—fighting back. While not all ways of fighting back are as impulsive as my reaction to the freeway bully or my attack on the high school football player, they all have in common the presumption that we must defend ourselves or we will be destroyed. "No one is going to take care of me because everyone is selfish; they are only concerned for themselves," might be an unstated motto for the combative option. There is a television program called *Fight Back,* where very assertive and aggressive steps are taken against merchants who have treated customers unjustly. Often the program directors threaten to take businesses to court if they do not right the wrongs they have committed. Much of the time this fighting back works. You can see the satisfaction in the faces of those who have won their arguments. They feel good about themselves again.

Sometimes labeled "standing up for your rights," this kind of self-defense can turn violent. A recent television news program told about a driver who had stopped another driver and accused her of endangering him by weaving in and out of lanes on the highway. When she didn't apologize, he broke her window and seized her purse. It reduced his angry feelings, but he later had to pay for her repairs!

When fighting back doesn't work, revenge sometimes takes over. Revenge involves the reclaiming of self esteem by attack after the offense has happened. Revenge is based on the presumption that others have intentionally taken away one's status by some form of trespass. Self-pride means that one cannot let the offense go without reacting to it. A response is demanded. If one does not react, then other people will assume that the offense and loss of self-esteem were justified.

There are two forms of revenge: retribution and retaliation. Retribution is the more elemental of the two. It is based on the "eye for an eye, tooth for a tooth" maxim. It is grounded in a distortion of the golden rule, "Do unto others *what* they have done to you." The presumption is that the only way to gain back lost self-esteem is by calling others the exact names one has been called, hitting them in the same places one has been hit, stealing from them what has been stolen, spreading the same rumors about them that they have spread, etc. Satisfaction comes from knowing that the other persons have not gotten away with the hurt and that the score has been settled; they have suffered in the same way that you have suffered.

Retribution is often thought of as the Old Testament law. It can be seen in the fabled feuds of mountaineers in the Appalachians where, if a person in one family is killed, a person from the other family will be killed in revenge. Gang wars in big cities sometimes reflect this same kind of thinking. Notice the way feuding families, criminals, or gang members talk about these actions. The emphasis is always on their "feelings" and their "pride." Retribution reduces the distressful feelings of conflict; it does not solve the problem. Feuds go on and on.

The second type of revenge is called retaliation. The major difference between retaliation and retribution is that, in retaliation, returning the injury in exactly the same manner in which it occurred is impossible or not sufficient. A good example is a traffic accident in which a loved one has been killed. It is impossible to run over the offending driver. Therefore, the only satisfaction that can be gained is to see that the driver is sentenced to jail. Mothers Against Drunk Driving (MADD) is an example of constructive retaliation.

Furthermore, jail may not seem adequate as a punishment for taking a life and a person may seek monetary recompense through a legal suit. These are examples of retaliation. More typical examples include attempting to get colleagues fired, spreading rumors, shunning those who offend us, and punishing persons in one way or another for what they have done.

A sad example of this is the case of Gary Coleman and his parents. Several years ago, Coleman, the long-time co-star of the TV program "Diff'rent Strokes," sued his parents for stealing close to $1 million from him. They countersued him for alleged defamation and breach of contract. This kind of tit-for-tat retaliation might make either side feel better, but it probably never solved their problems or brought them closer together.

These are but a few of the Defensive ways to reduce conflict. We turn next to the Conventional alternative.

Conventional Conflict Reduction

Earlier, I said that Conventional conflict reduction was grounded in an assumption that distress could be reduced if everybody calmed down and discussed problems rationally and dispassionately. Underneath this assumption was another, even more foundational, conviction that no one had intended to hurt anybody and there had been a misunderstanding that could be worked out if everyone would just sit down and clarify what had happened. Thus, since there is goodwill all around, there is no need to defend oneself in order to regain the status and identity that go into self-esteem. The Conventional approach assumes that nothing dangerous has occurred. There has simply been a misunderstanding that can be corrected by cool-headed, calm interaction.

An example on the international scene was the visit of former President Jimmy Carter to North Korea during a crisis over nuclear arms. In the midst of that country's seeming refusal to allow inspectors access to its facilities, the United States was ready to encourage the United Nations to take aggressive action to force North Korea into compliance by burdening them with trade sanctions. Carter was able to convince North Korea, and later the United States, to sit down for high-level talks in order to see if an agreement could not be reached. The assumption under this recommendation was that there had been a tragic misunderstanding but that neither country wanted to be an enemy of the other. Goodwill made the meeting possible. This was Conventional conflict reduction at its best. The pride and self-esteem of both countries were preserved. Feelings returned to normal optimism.

An example closer to home might be the situation in which a couple experiencing marital difficulties is compelled to go for six months of counseling before being given a divorce. Although such counseling does not always work, in many cases husbands and wives discover that hurt feelings were getting in their way of each other's basic commitment to the relationship. After they calm down, they are able to reclaim their love for each other and save their marriage by using Conventional ways of conflict reduction.

The word *accident* is often used to describe what we feel when we look at conflict through Conventional eyes. Accidents are just what the term implies—unintentional mishaps that can either be forgotten, forgiven, or fixed. On many occasions we have judged each other harshly only to find that there was a logical reason for what happened and that the harm that was done was not intended. People generally are not out to get us.

Many authors who write about conflict make Conventional assumptions about conflict. They assume that the dictionary definition of conflict is absolutely correct. The dictionary says that conflict is "two people trying to occupy the same space." In their recommendations about handling conflict, these writers suggest that persons put their feelings aside and sit down and talk with each other. An example might be the situation in which a group wanted to renovate a vacant building into apartments for homeless families. Many homeowners in the neighborhood were opposed because they thought that having the homeless so close would lower their property values. The community housing group that was proposing the plan took the Conventional option and called some community meetings to discuss the issues. They were confident that reasonable solutions could be found that would please everybody. They just needed to talk it through.

There are several aspects of the Conventional alternative. On the surface these resemble many of the steps in good problem solving. But it should be remembered that the primary goal of Conventional conflict reduction is lowering the feelings of distress people are having. When feelings become less angry, persons can return to the task of dealing with the problems over which they went into conflict. A lot of problem solving goes on in Conventional conflict reduction. However, calming down and reassuring each other of goodwill comes first. Solving problems comes second.

Conventional conflict reduction is grounded in a trust of the system. "Trusting the system" means having confidence that things work in the way things are supposed to work. All of society is based on the assumption that we can trust each other to abide by the rules of justice and fairness. When something goes awry the "system" concludes that an accident has occurred, that what happened was unplanned and unintentional, that the situation can be corrected if people will just talk it out or remind each other of the rules of justice and fairness.

For example, here in America we drive our cars on the right side of the road. When we see a car swerve over the center line as it comes toward us, we assume the driver has gone to sleep or become distracted. So we honk our horn and expect the car to straighten up and turn back to the right side of the street. Although we may not like it and may say to ourselves, "Why doesn't that driver watch where he's going," we do not assume that the driver was really trying to cause an accident.

The same thing is true when we buy something and it turns out to be of inferior quality. We don't assume that the merchant tried to swindle us. For example, I recently ordered an oboe reed from a store that sent it to me in the mail. When it came, however, the opening in the reed made it unplayable. With postage, the cost was almost twenty dollars. I called the store and told them that there was a problem with the reed. "Just send it back, and we'll send you another or return your money," the clerk said. I assumed that the store would play by the rules and they did.

A better personal example of the use of Conventional conflict reduction would be how I felt when they changed the code on the parking garage gates in the condominium complex where I live. The management company periodically changes the codes on the remote control devices we all use to open the gates to the underground parking garage. We lease our apartment, so we don't receive the notification that the codes have been changed; they are sent to the owner from whom we rent. The owner forgets to notify us so, at times, we have tried to get out of the garage and couldn't because our remote control devices had the outdated code. Fortunately, someone usually comes by and tells us what the new code is.

Each time we found that the code didn't work, we would call the owner and complain that she had not notified us. We would tell her our fear that there might be a time when we have an emergency and need to get to the hospital but might not be able to get out of the garage because we had not been told of a code change. Each time, she would apologize, but the same thing happens again.

I'm becoming increasingly frustrated with her. Yet, my intent is to keep calling her and insisting that she notify us of the changes. I am convinced that she is just forgetful and disorganized. I am bordering on becoming distressed, but I will not take any other kind of drastic action yet. I just may call her at midnight if that is the hour at which I next become frustrated, however!

Trusting the system has to be followed by assertion of oneself back into the relationship, as can be seen in my example of changing the code on the remote control device. Conventional conflict reduction will not work if it remains "arm chair" theorizing. In marriage counseling, I often say to the husband and wife, "Speak up! Tell the other person what bothers you and what you want in the relationship. Your spouse cannot read your mind!"

Just thinking that things will work out or that others will see the problem and correct it, won't work. If persons don't assert themselves, they will just get more angry, more anxious, and more distressed. A client of mine on welfare did not receive her monthly stickers for receiving medical care. She became frantic and called me for advice. She immediately assumed they were angry with her and were cutting off her assistance. I said, "Calm down. There has probably been a mistake. Maybe it got lost in the mail; give them a call." She did. They apologized and sent her replacement stickers in the next day's mail. Had she not asserted herself and made the call, her anxiety would have become intolerable.

After trusting the system and asserting oneself, the next step in Conventional conflict reduction is to remain rational. The Book of Proverbs is full of advice on how to do Conventional conflict reduction. Listen to some of these admonitions:

▼ "When words are many, sin is not absent, but he who holds his tongue is wise" (10:19).

▼ "A fool shows his annoyance at once, but a prudent man overlooks an insult" (12:16).

▼ "A gentle answer turns away wrath, but a harsh word stirs up anger" (15:1).

▼ "A hot-tempered man stirs up dissension, but a patient man calms a quarrel" (15:18).

▼ "Better a patient man than a warrior, a man who controls his temper than one who takes a city" (16:32).

▼ "He who answers before listening—that is his folly and his shame" (18:13).

▼ "It is to a man's honor to avoid strife, but every fool is quick to quarrel" (20:3).

▼ "A wicked man puts up a bold front, but an upright man gives thought to his ways" (21:29).

▼ "As charcoal to embers and as wood to fire, so is a quarrelsome man for kindling strife" (26:21).

▼ "A fool gives full vent to his anger, but a wise man keeps himself under control" (29:11).

Conventional conflict reduction works best when we really trust the system and assert ourselves in a calm and rational manner. This is often very difficult to do when we are in the distress of conflict; but it is possible if we can put into action what we say we really believe, namely, that other people can be trusted to have goodwill in their hearts toward us.

Transcendent Conflict Reduction

We turn now to the last of the three ways to reduce conflict. I have labeled this type of conflict reduction Transcendent but it could just as easily have been labeled "Religious," or "Christian," or "Spiritual." The core idea in Transcendent conflict reduction is to somehow surmount, get above, or transcend the situation so that distress feelings can disappear or become inconsequential. Paul states it well in Romans 12:2, "Be not conformed to this world: but be ye transformed by the renewing of your mind, that ye may prove what is that good, and acceptable, and perfect, will of God."

Almost all religions promise that this can happen, and many persons testify to spiritual resources that help them make it through the stress and distress of life. In fact, one definition of religion is that religion is the way people handle the tragedies, the travails, the mysteries, and the triumphs of life.

I am convinced that few transcendent resources for conflict reduction compare to those found in the Jewish/Christian tradition. A recent country song stated that "a country boy can survive." I'm convinced that "a Christian can survive" conflict. Jesus' encouragement to "Let not your heart be troubled; ye believe in God, believe also in me" (John 14:1) is an invitation that has been proven to be true again and again.

It is good to remind ourselves of some of these promises of security, comfort, and reassurance in the Psalms as we begin this discussion of Transcendent conflict reduction. All are from the *New International Version.*

▼ "You turned my wailing into dancing; you removed my sackcloth and clothed me with joy" (30:11).

▼ "Our help is in the name of the Lord, the Maker of heaven and earth" (124:8).

▼ "For you, O Lord, have delivered my soul from death, my eyes from tears, my feet from stumbling, that I may walk before the Lord in the land of the living" (116:8–9).

▼ "The Lord protects the simplehearted; when I was in great need, he saved me" (116:6).

▼ "If the Lord had not been on our side when men attacked us, when their anger flared against us, they would have swallowed us alive; the flood would have engulfed us, the torrent would have swept over us" (124:2–4).

▼ "When I called, you answered me; you made me bold and stouthearted. . . . Though I walk in the midst of trouble, you preserve my life" (138:3, 7).

▼ "Even though I walk through the valley of the shadow of death, I will fear no evil, for you are with me" (23:4).

▼ "You are my hiding place; you will protect me from trouble and surround me with songs of deliverance" (32:7).

▼ "Why are you downcast, O my soul? Why so disturbed within me? Put your hope in God" (42:11).

▼ "God is our refuge and strength, an ever-present help in trouble" (46:1).

▼ "Evening, morning and noon I cry out in distress, and he hears my voice" (55:17).

▼ "When I am afraid, I will trust in you" (56:3).

▼ "I will take refuge in the shadow of your wings until the disaster has passed" (57:1).

There are many more verses that attest to the amazing way that relating oneself to God in the midst of distress reduces anxiety and restores peace in one's heart. These are but a few of the examples of the promise that conflict feelings can be reduced through faith. Notice how vividly realistic are the words that these verses use to describe the emotions we are really feeling when we are in conflict and the power of God to soothe our anxieties and calm our fears.

How does this process occur? The steps in Christian Transcendent conflict reduction are *Remembrance, Reassurance, Repentance, and Reassertion.* These four steps are all based on the presumption that the basic thing that has caused us to go into conflict is that we have forgotten who we really are. We have falsely concluded that our self-esteem was based on what others thought of us; we have incorrectly assumed that our identity and status were based on our own achievements in life.

These false assumptions make us very vulnerable to those who might want to do us harm, as in the thought underlying Defensive conflict reduction, or to those who unintentionally but self-centeredly violate society's rules, as in the thought underlying Conventional conflict reduction.

Transcendent conflict reduction takes a neutral position about whether other persons are evil or not. It assumes there is a grandeur and a misery to human life. Persons can make mistakes; they can apologize and make things right; they can be gracious and compassionate and wonderful. At the same time, persons can be sinful and evil. They can set out to harm others; they can be selfish and possessive; they can intentionally hurt and destroy.

The basic thought that underlies Christian conflict reduction is that "God loves us." John 3:16 says it best: "For God so loved the world, that he gave his only begotten Son that whosoever believeth in him should not perish, but have everlasting life."

As the theologian Paul Tillich said in one of his powerful sermons, "You are accepted: *You are accepted!*" This does not mean we, or others, are "acceptable." It does mean that God loves and accepts us in spite of our sinfulness. As someone said, "I'm not OK. You're not OK. But that's OK." The question of whether we should have good self-esteem has been settled once and for all by Jesus' death and resurrection.

We need not be fearful, anxious, or distressed because, as Paul said in quoting Hosea: "'Those who were not my people I will call "my people," and she who was not beloved I will call "my beloved." And in every place where it was said to them, "You are not my people," they will be called the "sons of the living God""' (Rom. 9:25–26, RSV). We need not worry any more. Our self-esteem is not up for grabs in the latest confrontation. Nor is it subject to the latest whims of popularity. We can rest secure.

The great western pioneer Horace Greeley put it well when he said, "Fame is a vapor, popularity is an accident, riches take wings, those who cheer today will curse tomorrow." We will always be vulnerable to going into conflict if we put our trust in these. In fact, putting our trust in these things is due to our failure to remember that we are loved by God. That can quiet our souls. The prophet Isaiah assures us that "Thou wilt keep him in perfect peace, whose mind is stayed on thee" (Isa. 26:3).

▼

Steps in Transcendent Conflict Reduction

Step 1: Remembrance—An act of the mind, remembering who and whose we are.
▼
Step 2: Reassurance—An act of the heart, reassuring ourselves of the truths of our faith.
▼
Step 3: Repentance—Repentance for our behavior to our brothers and sisters when we are in conflict is not an option
▼
Step 4: Reassertion—Reassert ourselves back into the problem over which we went into conflict.
▼

So the first step in Transcendent conflict reduction is Remembering who, and whose, we are. We belong to God; we are precious in His sight; He has settled once and for all time the question of our self-worth. Therefore, we can have high self-esteem; we can think well of ourselves and not become distressed because God loves and treasures us.

Remembrance must be followed by Reassurance. Remembrance is an act of the mind; Reassurance is an act of the heart. We all know the difference between these two. We can read verses of Scripture and recall the great promises of Jesus, the psalmist, the prophets, and the apostle Paul. They become reminders to us of the truths of God's love. But unless they seep down from the top of our heads to the depths of our hearts, they become as "water off a duck's back" when we experience distress again.

We need to reassure ourselves of the truths of our faith. Christians do this by prayer. They take the time to wait on God in silence and to make the simple, but profound, request, "Oh Lord, make the truths of the Bible become the truths of my heart."

When the step of Reassurance is not taken, we may go back into conflict, as the following illustration shows. I once became very distressed over a problem with one of my colleagues. For many months I had hateful, evil thoughts about her. She had treated me unjustly, and I wanted to see her suffer. I believed all the gossip I heard about her and encouraged those who disliked her and wanted to see her fired. I voted against anything she favored.

One day in my devotions I woke up to what I was doing. I realized that I was in conflict over the situation and that I had become combative in the way that I was handling my feelings. In reading the Bible I became aware that I had given over to her my self-esteem. I reminded myself of my security in God and immediately felt better. Quickly, I wrote a note to her confessing my ill will and asking for a renewed relationship.

Several weeks passed with no response. Finally, a note appeared in my mailbox. It read, "I don't know what I can do to help you with your problem." I became angry and distressed all over again. I went back into conflict for several more months. My problem was that I had remembered but not reassured myself that my self-esteem really depends on God. When my colleague did not act lovingly toward me, I became consumed with hurt all over again instead of settling down in the assurance of God's love. I had not taken the time to reassure myself through prayer.

To those of us in the Methodist tradition, this difference between head and heart knowledge is a familiar theme. Our founder, John Wesley, had been a priest in the Church of England for over a decade before he had his heart-warming experience. It was only after this event that he stated, "I did truly know my sins forgiven." He was constantly searching for "assurance" of God's grace during all these years that he was still actively engaged in full-time religious work. He had head knowledge but not heart knowledge; he had Remembrance but not Reassurance. Thus, the second step is Reassurance.

The third step is Repentance. Repentance for what? Several things. First, repentance is needed for forgetting that we are creations of God, precious in His sight. It is so easy to forget where our real worth lies. It is amazingly tempting to judge ourselves on what we can see, smell, touch, hear, and taste—the five senses. It is very human, and very sinful, to come to the realization that we have been deeply upset and anxious because we didn't win an argument or because we were ignored or mistreated by others. We need to acknowledge our frailty and our forgetfulness. We need to ask for God's forgiveness and commit ourselves to better memory. We need to truthfully acknowledge that in comparison to God's love for us, nothing else in life matters! In a somewhat humorous vein, we need to reassert what the comedian Flip Wilson used to say was the theme of his "Church of What's Happening Now," namely, "It don't matter!" And in absolute truth, nothing else does matter. For as Paul states in the powerful words of Romans 8:38–39, "For I am persuaded, that neither death, nor life, nor angels, nor principalities, nor powers, nor things present, nor things to come, nor height, nor depth, nor any other creature, shall be able to separate us from the love of God, which is in Christ Jesus our Lord." We need to repent for forgetting this.

The reaction to my seminary colleague typifies the second thing for which we should be repentant. I hated my colleague and treated her as if she were worthless, as if she had no value, as if our seminary would be better off if she would leave.

Jesus reminds us in Matthew 5:22 that "whosoever shall say, Thou fool, shall be in danger of hell fire." In effect, I treated my colleague as a fool, a person without sense or worth. The Scripture implies that this kind of sin is almost unforgivable. It is almost the worst thing that we can do. To act toward another person as if they are worthless is almost like saying that one of God's creations should not have been born. Because each one of us is precious in God's eyes and Christ died for every person, to act as I did toward my colleague was a grievous sin.

I am convinced that I am not alone. We do tend to personalize problems and identify problems with people. Of all that frustrates us in life, nothing frustrates us like other people. So the temptation to oppose, attack, and even destroy each other when we become distressed is understandable, even if it is almost unforgivable. Repentance for our behavior toward our brothers and sisters when we are in conflict is not an option. We need to reflect on what we have done—by thought, by word, by deed—and ask God's forgiveness.

There is a third thing for which we should routinely repent when we utilize Transcendent conflict reduction. We should repent for thinking that we are *absolutely* correct in our point of view. Since people go into conflict over problems, in almost every case we will have taken a position in opposition to someone else. In debates, for example:

▼ over the textbooks to be used in a school;

▼ over charges on a credit card;

▼ over repairs on an automobile;

▼ over whether a professor is true to the Bible;

▼ over how money from an estate will be divided;

▼ over who is responsible for an accident; and

▼ over whether or not a friend cheated in a transaction.

In all of these situations there are at least two sides to the argument. As part of God's creation, we are held responsible for having an opinion and taking a stand. That is God's will. We will not always be wrong—nor will we always be right!

In using the Transcendent way to reduce conflict, we should not feel obligated to repent because we had an opinion. Nor are we obligated to back down and give in. We should, however, be willing to reflect a bit on the stand we have taken. There is always the possibility, even the probability, that as we move from the stress of problem solving to the distress of conflict, we will overstate our case. We need to repent for the ways in which we exaggerated the rightness of our point of view and our unwilling-ness to see other points of view and moderate our position.

For example, in the case where I was at odds with my faculty colleague, I had to admit that when I used the Transcendent way to reduce conflict, she had a point when she said that I had offended her. The issue was not as one-sided as I had claimed. We had been writing a book together and she was convinced that I had not been pulling my weight. I denied this vehemently. However, she was right; I had been derelict. I needed to repent and to acknowledge that the issue was not entirely one-sided.

Having repented of our forgetfulness of God's love, our hatred of another person, and our overstatement of our point of view, the final step in Transcendent conflict reduction is to reassert ourselves back into the problem over which we went into conflict. If we do not do this, we might as well be Buddhist. Buddhism denies the reality of this world's problems. Christians cannot do that. This is God's good creation and we Christians are to be active in ensuring "the kingdoms of this world become the kingdom of our Lord and of his Christ" (Rev. 11:15). Solving problems is the will of God for Christians. They cannot step aside and simply enjoy the love God has for them without being involved in the issues of life.

Of course, reducing conflict feelings so that persons can return to the stress of problem solving is the goal of all three types of conflict reduction. Defensive, Conventional, and Transcendent approaches share this common goal. However, reasserting oneself back into the issues is a special mandate in the Christian method because *reassertion* is seen as the will of God. Because persons have remembered who they are, reassured themselves of their status and identity in God's eyes, and repented of their sins, they can confidently return to the problems of life and use their reasonable minds to seek solutions that are good for everyone involved.

This chapter has described the three basic methods for conflict reduction: Defensive, Conventional, and Transcendent. There are good and bad aspects to each of them. I do not mean to say that being Defensive is always bad; it is sometimes good because there is evil out there in the world. Having enough self-respect to stand up and fight or to surrender when the odds are overwhelming may be the best thing to do sometimes. In general, the Conventional method will work much of the time;

and it is probably good to give it a chance. The Transcendent way is always appropriate, particularly in times of great distress and high threat. All in all, each and every option should be considered. The most effective conflict reduction often will be a combination of the three approaches.

I close this chapter with yet another case study. It is called "We Deserve to Suffer" and is about a crisis that arose in a Sunday School class. Try your hand at thinking through how the conflict feelings the people are experiencing might be reduced by listing what they could do if the Defensive, the Conventional, or the Transcendent method was used. Then go back through what you have written and decide on the best combination of the three methods. Assume that you are Claire Bronson, the director of Christian Education.

▼

WE DESERVE TO SUFFER

Claire Bronson could not believe what happened in the single young adult Sunday School class yesterday. "I suppose I should rejoice when persons take the lesson seriously enough to have strong feelings about it," she mused to herself as she reflected on the event, "but Anita sure got into it. There must have been something else going on for her to get so overwrought over whether we deserve to suffer or not. I think I know what's happening. I know her pretty well."

Background

For about six weeks, Claire Bronson, director of Christian education at Knox Presbyterian Church, has been teaching the single young adult Sunday School. The class has been reading Lewis Smedes' book *Love Within Limits*. Yesterday's lesson had to do with suffering, and the Scripture the class was considering was 1 Corinthians 13. There was a discussion of whether humans are victims or whether they deserve to suffer. The class has ten members, most of whom are regular attenders. Those who did the most talking yesterday were Anita, Frank, and Marcia.

Frank is divorced from his second marriage. On several occasions he has shared with the class that discussions about love are painful to him because of his marital failures. He reacted defensively when Anita stated that humans always deserve to suffer. He didn't agree.

Marcia has had a great many health problems, both physical and mental. She has been in a weekly Bible study with several of the other women in the class. Anita organized the class and has been leading it. When Anita asserted that God intends that people should suffer, Marcia reacted strongly. This was not the God she knows and loves. It would be hard for her to agree that her suffering was willed by God.

Anita's background is Catholic. She reports that she became a "real" Christian in college through an Intervarsity Fellowship group. She can quote Scripture eloquently and is quite dogmatic in her outlook. In reaction to Smedes' contention in Love Within Limits that people are often victims of others' wrongdoings when they suffer, Anita had objected. She firmly stated that, "People deserve to suffer."

Christian Education Director Bronson has spent much counseling time with all three of these class members. As she mused over yesterday's class meeting, she remembered each of them. She remembered the pain Frank suffered when his second marriage failed. She comforted him and tried to work for reconciliation.

She remembered many visits with Marcia as she struggled to regain her strength after mononucleosis and a bout with depression. She knew that Marcia was plagued with self-doubt as well as stubborn tenacity.

Anita had a difficult time adjusting to the Presbyterian church. It lacked the enthusiasm of her college Intervarsity experience, and many of its practices didn't seem to Anita to be biblically based. Furthermore, the congregation seemed to be far too liberal in their beliefs. Yet Claire Bronson had convinced Anita that there was a place for her at the church, and she felt comfortable most of the time. Yet at other times she felt strangely alone.

Predicament

During the class discussion yesterday, Anita spoke up and said she disagreed that most people who suffer are victims.

"We are not victims. We deserve to suffer. Look at the story of the fall in Genesis. God banished Adam and Eve from the Garden of Eden and told them their lives would be full of suffering. Because of the fall we are all condemned to suffer. We deserve to suffer as a punishment for our sins," Anita stated firmly. There was no sign of doubt or ambivalence in her voice.

Frank replied quickly: "Hey, I am a sinner; with that I agree. But I don't take responsibility for Adam and Eve. I do not suffer because of what they did. I agree that sometimes I cause my own suffering. However, there are many times when I am not to blame. At times I am an innocent victim."

Marcia remained quiet. She looked down at the floor and said nothing.

Christian Education Director Bronson laughed nervously as she saw the tension mount. "Well, let's not get into a discussion of Genesis right now," she suggested. She tried to support Anita in her recognition of corporate sinfulness but also affirmed that it is hard to see ourselves as always deserving the suffering we experience. "I just cannot believe that those around us who suffer more than others always deserve it," Bronson continued. This was her way of supporting Frank and Marcia.

Other class members joined in with Frank and confronted Anita. Anita was becoming increasingly isolated, however. There was the chance that she might feel rejected. Claire

Bronson attempted once again to lift up the positive value in Anita's position.

However, her efforts went unheeded because by this time Anita had checked out of the class discussion and was interacting with a friend of hers who was visiting the class that Sunday. Whereas before this she had sat forward on her seat and actively participated in the debate, she was now whispering and laughing with her friend as they discussed the situation. Claire Bronson saw her cast a glance at Frank and wrinkle her nose in a sneer as if to say that he and the rest of the class were not "real" Christians because the Bible clearly implies that humans deserve suffering.

At the end of the class, Claire stated, "We come together to study and struggle with God's Word for us. Often we bring different experiences and perceptions to this task. What is important is that we can share these differences in love. We may never completely agree, but hopefully we grow in our journey of faith together."

She was not sure that Anita heard or agreed with her. Anita seemed very distressed as she left without speaking to anyone.

"What more could I have done? What should I do now?" These are the questions in Claire Bronson's mind as she thinks of yesterday's single young adult Sunday School class meeting.

▼

CHAPTER FIVE

Conflict reduction
begins with you

▼

We have met the enemy, and they are us.
— Pogo

▼

This comment by the creator of Pogo about the enemy should become a first-step maxim for all Christians who want to prevent war from breaking out when conflict occurs. The first enemy to confront is ourselves.

Matthew 7:3–5 reminds us how easy it is to observe the "mote" in another's eye while ignoring the "beam" in our own. It is tempting and easy to forget that "beams" in our own eyes distort vision just as much as "motes" do in others' eyes. Jesus cautioned us to be hesitant to judge others before we examine ourselves. Only after self-reflection did He conclude we would be able to "see clearly" what was really happening.

Seeing clearly what is happening inside oneself is an absolute necessity for those who would reduce conflict in themselves and solve the problems of life. Problems will never be solved half as well as long as even one person is in conflict. We should never forget that we will tend to deny our distress and focus on the problem we are facing rather than the feelings we are having. Our convictions about the rightness of our opinions and the wrongness of the opposition overshadow the truth that we are letting our pride and our self-esteem foul up our reactions. There truly are "beams" in our eyes that distort our perceptions.

More often than not these beams in our eyes are only indirectly related to the problem we are trying to settle. Like a spark that sets off a brush fire, our feelings about ourselves sweep us along and color our interactions to the point that we begin to behave automatically and impulsively.

Anyone who has ever watched movies of Hitler's harangues and the reaction of the crowds knows what I'm referring to. People seem to be easily caught up with the emotions of the moment and the threats they feel to their pride and self-esteem. Far too easily, people passionately place the blame entirely on those who they call their enemies. The Germans under the Nazi regime are only a vivid illustration of what most persons do when they are in conflict.

And this kind of thinking was not confined to Hitler's Germany. Even American Christians got in on the act. The pastor of Plymouth Congregational Church in Brooklyn spoke the feelings of many when he recommended complete extermination of the German people. He publicly approved of a plan to sterilize German soldiers and isolate German women so that the nation would be destroyed in one generation. Although his statements were made with reference to Germany in the First World War, many will agree that his ideas would probably apply even more strongly to what was said during the Second World War—by otherwise very religious persons!

Jesus knew how easy it is to fall into such outlandish behavior. Vision becomes blurred in the heat of the battle. Wars begin when protagonists fail to search their own eyes for "beams" before they attack the "motes" in others. Modern psychologists call Jesus' observation "the danger of projection"—blaming someone else for that of which you yourself are guilty.

Projection is a dangerous example of farsightedness; being unable to see things nearby while being perfectly clear about what lies in the distance. Correcting one's vision through self-reflection is an absolutely essential step for those who would see clearly. Only when vision is clear is there any remote chance of handling conflict without going to war.

A Personal Illustration

I recently went through an experience that illustrates the ease with which we can sink into farsighted projection. Like a magnet attracting iron filings, projection of the blame and responsibility onto others when a problem arises can seem like an almost irresistible temptation.

The situation was this. I am a member of a graduate faculty in psychology. I differed with a colleague over a grade he had given one of my advisees. I did not realize until it was too late that I had gone into conflict over the situation. My feelings of antagonism toward him became consuming. I began to role play the arguments I would use when next I saw him. I started to believe negative rumors I had heard about his style of teaching. As I went to sleep I would replay the situation and further elaborate my opinions about why I disapproved of his behavior. I was in conflict; I was distressed.

I confronted him. I told him that I had been at the school for twenty-four years and that I knew our philosophy. I insinuated that he was an upstart who was trying to change things and teach us old-timers a lesson. He said he thought I was condescending. Pridefully, I agreed, thinking that this young professor needed to learn a thing or two. I told him I had heard nothing but complaints about him, which was an exaggeration of the truth.

Only after I had allowed my anger to let me say more than I should have said, did I stop and reflect. I concluded that I was not just trying to solve a problem; I was in conflict over the grade he had given my advisee. I had behaved in a drastic manner. I had personally attacked him and threatened his position.

Before you challenge me, let me say that there was a real issue here. He had, in my opinion, graded my advisee unfairly and treated her unjustly. He had, indeed, pompously set out to teach the rest of us a lesson on toughness. He was a smart-aleck upstart. I was facing a real problem. And the problem did not change just because I admitted to myself that I was in conflict. What did change was my self awareness. What was different was my conviction that I could not solve the problem as long as I was in conflict.

Upon reflection, it became clear to me that I had allowed this grading problem to set off in me some feelings of desperation that predated my difficulty with him and were basically unrelated to the grade he gave my advisee. As I thought about my confrontation of my young colleague, which, incidentally did not provoke him to change the student's grade, I had to confess that I was already upset about my status in the faculty long before this problem arose.

At the time this situation occurred, I had just returned from being away for two years on sabbatical leave and as a visiting professor in another state. I was wondering whether I would be accepted back into the faculty after having been away so long. More than one person had mistakenly assumed I was not returning. Many acted surprised to see me back. After all, the faculty had been able to run the program very well without me for two years, and I fantasized they would just ignore me. I thought they were doing just that, ignoring me. I was the oldest member of the faculty, and it was known that I would be retiring very soon anyway. On top of that, I had been replaced in a central role that I had played and was simply being allowed to teach whatever courses I chose. I fantasized that I was just being tolerated until retirement and that I only had lame-duck power.

When the young professor did not immediately take my advice and change the grade of my advisee, I allowed the situation to push me over the line from stress to distress. I went into conflict. I even said to myself, "I cannot allow this youngster to get away with defying me; I must exert my power over him or I will lose my self-respect." A clearer illustration of being in conflict, I cannot imagine!

Now, the issue became clear to me: if I really wanted to reach the best solution to the problem I was having with my colleague, I had to be out of conflict. I had to be able to remain calm no matter how unjustly I felt he had behaved toward the student or how compassionate I felt toward her plight. I came to the realization that I had to keep the issue of his grades at the problem level in order for us to reach an equitable and fair solution to the problem. I realized I could only do this if I were out of conflict myself. It became clear to me that if I remained in conflict, my prime goal would remain one of trying to regain my self-esteem even though it might look like I was simply being firm and direct in my interaction with him. Further, if I remained in conflict, I would easily and impulsively become aggressive rather than assertive. I would tend to behave so rashly that I would run the risk of being the cause of his going into conflict, and if that happened we would have a war on our hands. I realized that I had to begin with myself and do whatever it took to get myself out of conflict.

Does My Experience Ring a Bell with You?

Hopefully, you can identify enough with this illustration to recall times when you, too, were in conflict even though you might not have recognized it at the time. Hopefully, you are able to recall times when, had you realized what was happening, the solution to whatever problem you were facing would have been greatly improved had you gotten yourself out of conflict. Things would have turned out better had you been stressed, but not *distressed*. The lesson to be learned is, "We must begin with ourselves." As the old spiritual states, "It's me, It's me, Oh Lord, standing in the need of prayer. Not my brother, not my sister, but me, Oh Lord, standing in the need of prayer."

So, the first question to be asked in any situation is "Am I in conflict?" And if the answer to that question is yes, then you should take the time to reduce your inner conflict before anything else is done.

How to Begin: Withdraw into Your Closet

Although Jesus was not directly referring to conflict in the sixth chapter of Matthew, conflict may well be one of those times when the admonition to "enter into thy closet" (Matt. 6:6) should be the path to take. To "enter into thy closet" obviously means to get offstage, to withdraw from the battle, to go where nobody else can see or interrupt you. That is what it takes to determine whether you need to reduce the conflict in yourself. While facing yourself and deciding whether you are in conflict can be done in the midst of problem solving, it is much easier to do when you are alone.

I have found that getting myself out of conflict is something I, personally, can never do in public. Sometimes I have tried, but it has never worked. Only when I have gone into my "closet" have

I found it possible to do the hard work of thinking that is necessary to stop myself from warmongering.

Jesus knew how easy it is to get drawn into protecting our pride and how difficult to get in touch with our own distress when we remain outside the room where problems are being debated.

Once you are in your closet, my first recommendation is, "Shut the door!" You may react quickly and protest, "But it's dark in here; I can't see a thing." That is exactly what's intended. If you turn on the light or crack the door, you will be distracted by what is hanging in the closet or by the noise of what is still going on in the room. Forcing yourself to shut out all the light will guarantee that you have to look inside, rather than outside, yourself. Self-examination is hard work. We don't like to do it; it is an unwelcome task. It can never be done well when there is the slightest crack in the closet door that will let in outside light to distract us.

Tools for the Look Inside

The stress-distress line is not a wall that people climb over and know they have done it because they are out of breath. The stress-distress line is like a morning mist that easily turns into a fog bank. People are in it before they know it. They suddenly realize that they can no longer see, and they wonder what has happened.

Yes, reflecting on one's inner conflict state is like finding one's way out of a fog bank. What is needed is a set of tools for self-examination that will keep us from getting further confused. The tools I am going to suggest make it possible to retrace the steps that led us up to crossing the line from problem solving to conflict, from stress to distress. Like rethinking how one got from morning mist to fog bank, they help us decide whether, and to what extent, we have gone into conflict over the problems we were facing.

There are several tool-like guidelines for looking inside oneself. The Few or Many guideline helps us count the number of stresses we are experiencing at a given moment. The Now and Then guideline helps us make sense of why we have become so upset over this issue at this particular time. The More or Less guideline helps us take our "conflict temperature" and decide how much threat we are feeling—just a little or very, very much. The In and Out guideline helps us reflect on whether and why we have fluctuated and come out of, or gone into, conflict from moment to moment. Finally, the Yes or No guideline helps us sum up our thinking about all the other guidelines and make a final judgment about our state of mind. Let's consider each of these guidelines in turn.

Tools for an Inside Look

1. *Few or Many:* How many other stresses am I facing right now that might make me more vulnerable to going into conflict?

▼

2. *Now and Then:* Sometimes I do and sometimes I don't go into conflict over the same situation.

▼

3. *More or Less:* To what extent am I distressed because the issue is, or is not, important to me?

▼

4. *In and Out:* Has there ever been a time during problem solving when I went into, but came out of, conflict?

▼

5. *Yes and No:* Taking everything into consideration, am I in conflict or not?

▼

Few or Many

There is a rule that says, "The greater number of stresses people face, the more likely they will go into conflict over the next problem they face." There is nothing profound about this maxim. It is a restatement of the old adage that a final straw will break a camel's back. You can load a camel down with an immense load, but there comes a time when even adding one straw will be sufficient to break the camel's back. So it is with human beings. We speak of people having a "plate full" of trouble. Like camels, people can only stand so much stress, only so many problems to be solved, only so much threat to their self-esteem.

A friend of mine went back to work when she was forty years old. Her marriage had broken up six months earlier, and she had finally come out of the depression that oppressed her after it was all over. She had a hard time finding a job because she had been a stay-at-home mother during the eighteen years of her marriage. Finally, she landed a job at the city library.

Things went well the first year. However, in late summer of her second year a new director of the library was hired. He was just out of graduate school, young enough to be her son and very authoritative. She felt unable to please him. Her husband was behind in his alimony payments, and she was having a hard time making ends meet. In addition, her oldest daughter announced that she wanted to get married. While she was trying to deal with all these pressures, her teenage son broke his leg at football practice. Finally, a storm blew off some roof shingles which caused a leak.

When she went into work the next day, the director called her into his office and accused her of leaving early the night before. Her face flushed, and she became very angry. Sobbing, she told him off, and stormed out of his office without answering his accusation.

Here was a clear case where she had passed from the mist of problem stress into the fog of conflict because of the number of situations she was trying to deal with at that time. Note that until the director called her into his office, she was handling her problems as "problems." She was not in conflict. In fact, her daughter's forthcoming marriage was a pleasant problem. She loved her future son-in-law. If she had only had a few less stresses to deal with in her life at that moment, she might have stayed out of conflict.

My friend illustrates what we all have experienced. One more thing happens, and we lose our cool! One more problem breaks our ability to cope; a straw breaks the camel's back. The more stress we are in, the more vulnerable we are.

The first guideline, therefore, is to retrace our steps, think about all the things that are going on in our lives, and count the problems we are facing. Recognize that we may be distressed more because of the number of problems that we are trying to manage at a particular moment, than because of the importance of any one particular situation. My friend, for example, had already planned to join a group of other employees who were going to complain to the city council about the morale problem caused by the new director. She fully anticipated that he would change his ways or be fired. Neither her job nor her reputation was really at stake.

As you think about yourself, stop and consider the number of stresses you are facing at this moment. Make a list and total up the number of problems. To what extent are you vulnerable because of the Few or Many rule?

 Put the book down and follow the instructions.

Now and Then

The illustration of my friend who lambasted the library director leads easily into the second type of tool for self-examination, namely, the Now and Then guideline. If we stop and think, I am sure that we are just as familiar with Now and Then as we are with Few or Many. Put in a phrase, the Now and Then rule says, "Sometimes we do, and sometimes we don't" go into conflict over the same situation. Doesn't this surprise you to realize that we don't always get upset about the same thing? Some days we do, and some days we don't.

The emphasis here is less on the *number* of stresses in our lives and more on the type of stress that we are under at a given moment. PMS (premenstrual syndrome), which many women experience, is but an example of the type of vulnerability that occurs at one time, but not at another. Men, also, have their times. Their moods swing, too. It is a well-known fact in the psychology of selling that salesmen need to chart and monitor their "down times" during the month. They are encouraged to avoid business deals when they feel discouraged.

Not only does the time of *month*, but the time in *life* determines whether we will go into conflict over the stress of problem solving. My distress with my colleague over the grade he gave my advisee is a perfect example of the Now and Then guideline. My being near retirement and toward the end of my career made me vulnerable to becoming conflicted over something I would have handled as just a problem at another time in my life.

So, the Now and Then tool for self-examination helps us look at where we are in our lives. What types of stresses are we experiencing? Where are we in our life-struggle? What is happening to us health-wise? job-wise? money-wise? relationship-wise? hope-wise? family-wise? Being frank with ourselves about how susceptible we are at a given moment will help us realize that we bring certain life experiences to problem solving that may cause us to become distressed more easily at one time than another.

The crucial thing to realize is that the kind of predicament we are in at a given moment may predispose us to going into conflict over an issue we would have treated rationally at another time. The humorous way that women ask each other if they are having a "bad hair day" is illustrative of this truth. The "downsizing" which is going on in many companies leaves workers very vulnerable to becoming upset about work problems they would have handled in a reasonable fashion only a few months before. The fear of losing one's income is extremely stressful.

A policeman I once knew had a long record of excellent service. However, he was diagnosed as having leukemia at age forty-two. Treatment made the cancer go into remission, but the strain and worry left him feeling exhausted and anxious. He became quick tempered at work. As time went on his coworkers noted that he seemed lethargic at times and overly excitable at others. He finally decided to apply for disability—not because of the cancer, which was in remission, but because of underlying distress that had left him unable to handle the stress of everyday police work.

What is going on in your life today? Are you more vulnerable to going into conflict because of the type of problems you are facing? Take the time to reflect on your life and make a list of the types of stresses you are experiencing. Rate them along a 1–10 continuum, where 10 indicates extremely important and critical issues. See if you are carrying around feelings that will cause you to overreact to the next problem you face.

 Put the book down and follow the instructions.

More or Less

Not all issues are the same. Some situations are more important than others. For example, my youngest son said to his wife and children, "I've been down to the car dealer. You go and pick out the car. I don't care about the model or the color. The only thing is, I think it should hold all of us comfortably. They're expecting you." My youngest grandson chose the hunter green color; and my oldest grandson chose the model, a mini-van. I strongly doubt that these would have been the choices of my son, but it wasn't important enough for him to get upset about. He did not go into conflict over the model or the color of the new car.

Now, on another matter he lost his cool. His two young boys got in a fight one night as they were getting ready for bed. They had taken a bath together, then drew straws to see who would have to get out of the tub first. The one who drew the longest straw had the right to stay in the tub the longest. The youngest drew the short straw and began to cry. When asked what was the matter, he replied, "He called me a name." The truth was that he was furious that he lost the decision about getting out of the tub first. He and his brother had been roughhousing, but no name calling had occurred.

His father, my son, became very upset that his child would not be a good sport—a lesson that he had been trying to teach his children. He pulled his son out of the tub and angrily wiped him dry while chastising him severely. Because being a good sport was very important to him, he became much more upset than he did about the color and model of the car, an issue about which he cared little.

Thus, the question persons should ask of themselves is "To what extent am I distressed because the issue is, or is not, important to me?" There are two things to remember when answering this question about importance. First, *importance* usually means, "The issue affects my self-esteem." Second, sometimes we think something might endanger our self-esteem when it does not. No doubt, my son felt his reputation as a father would be threatened if his child did not show that he had learned how to be a good sport. This was probably an exaggeration. The situation was not as crucial as it seemed. The children had played well together up to that point, and the crisis was simply an exception to the rule. My son became threatened and anxious when he should not have been.

What needs to be remembered, however, about the More or Less guideline is that some problems upset us more than others. While we need to examine our feelings to see how realistic they are, there are, indeed, times when issues are crucial to who we see ourselves to be. Not all issues can be defused simply by saying, "I got too upset about a trivial matter."

Nevertheless, it should be remembered that it will be easier to get ourselves back from the distress of conflict to the stress of problem solving if we are less, rather than more, upset. Recognizing the degree of distress we are experiencing is a worthy task. It is tantamount to assessing our "conflict temperature." At least we know whether we are dealing with a mild sickness or a serious disease.

It is helpful to remember that the Now and Then maxim referred to *the underlying stress we bring to the problem* we are facing while the More or Less rule refers to *the importance of the problem itself.* For example, being worried about one's health might make someone go into conflict over a flat tire when before, they would have simply called the automobile club to come for help. That is the Now and Then rule. However, trying to settle the issue of whether or not to support the establishment of a homeless shelter next door when one is trying to sell the house may cause one to go into much greater distress than working on a committee to decide who will be hired as church organist.

Realizing that problems differ in importance might make us go more deeply into conflict without being aware of what is happening to us. Admitting that the stakes are higher on some issues than others is important. Knowing this can help us prepare for facing the problems. There is no doubt that after we cross the line from stress to distress it is still possible to be in conflict to a more or less degree. It is like swimming in a river. You can be distressed a little as you stand near the shore, or you can swim out in the main current and be swept away before you know it. Stop and look at the problems you are facing at this moment in your life. Are some of them more critical to you than others? Take note of those over which, should you become distressed, you would be more likely than others to go out into the deep water.

 Put the book down and follow the instructions.

In and Out

The next tool for self-examination is termed In and Out. Using this tool is a bit tricky. It involves thinking back over a given situation to see if there were times—during problem solving—when you went into, but came out of, conflict. Take the mist/fog bank analogy I described earlier. I inferred that going into conflict was like driving down the road and becoming aware that the windshield was clouding up with mist. Then, a few minutes later, it was like realizing that the mist seemed to have turned to fog and that the road ahead had disappeared from view. But, then you became aware that every now and then the fog cleared. Road signs could be seen; the way would suddenly become clear. Even the mist would go away like a puff of smoke. Then, all of a sudden, the fog would return, then go away again—unpredictably, intermittently.

This is what is meant by the Now and Then rule. A fog bank appears, and the distress of conflict comes over us. It comes and goes, often during the same hour as we try to solve the same problem. We go in and out of conflict.

If drivers were to use the In and Out tool to make sense of this situation, they would retrace their routes and try to determine what was happening when the fog lifted and what was happening when it returned. They would know that something was going on that made driving easier at one time than another.

Doing In and Out self-examination follows the same process. In thinking back over a stressful situation, persons might ask themselves the question, "Were there times when I lost my self-control and felt greatly disturbed?" Moreover, "Were there times when I was perfectly in control and feeling good?" The answers to these questions help persons know whether they had gone in and out of conflict as they tried to deal with the stress of handling their problems. Most importantly, they might be able to identify what combination of thoughts, feelings, actions, and interactions were occurring when their mood changed.

I remember a time when I was the pastor of a small church and lived in a run-down parsonage. We had Church School classes in every room of the house except our personal bedroom. The floor of the porch was rotten. My wife, who was pregnant at the time, fell through the porch steps on one occasion. We needed a new place to live. A house about a block away was for sale. I desperately wanted the church to buy it. The night the trustees took a vote I argued long and hard for buying the house. At times during the evening, I felt that several board members appreciated what I was saying. I kept my cool and discussed the matter calmly. But at other times, I felt the argument go the other way. I then became emotional. I went in and out of conflict all in the same evening. After the meeting, I found myself still trying to convince the group of my position. Then the chairman said, "Pastor, I'm not sure you realize it, but we just took a vote, and you were the only one voting to buy the house!" I was still in conflict and didn't realize the vote had been taken and the issue had been settled!

The goal of all this self-analysis is to get oneself out of conflict so that problems can be solved rationally instead of emotionally. The insights obtained by using the In and Out tool will help a person understand what they need to keep their self-esteem in good shape. We should never lose sight of where our self-esteem is at a given time. If we can determine those moments when we slip over from stress to distress, we can also forestall those moments by preparing for them ahead of time. Take a moment to reflect upon a time when you were trying to solve a problem. What were the signals that caused you to go in and out of conflict as you tried to deal with the stress of the situation?

 Put the book down and follow the instructions.

Yes and No

This final tool is like pieces of a jigsaw puzzle. Like the various parts of the puzzle, taken by themselves the several tools for self-examination may not make a complete picture. What is needed is some overall judgment about whether, and to what extent, we are in conflict. If we are, we need to reduce our inner conflict so we can avoid war and do good problem solving. If we are not, we can vigorously assert ourselves into the problems we are facing with the confidence that our inner conflict will not interfere with our reaching good solutions.

So the Yes and No process is one in which we step back and answer the question, "Taking everything into consideration, am I in conflict or not?" Further, "Adding up my judgments about the Few or Many, Now and Then, More or Less, and In and Out rules, what do I conclude? Do I need to deal with *myself* before I deal with the *problem* I am facing? Knowing what I now know, should I spend time reducing the distress I am feeling before I open my closet door and face other people?"

I can illustrate how I used these tools in my self-examination of my conflict state when I had the problem with my colleague over the grade he had given my advisee.

Few or Many: I was not under many other stresses at the time. My health was good. I was relaxed. I had just returned from two enjoyable years away. My wife and I had found a lovely condo in which to live. My car was not running smoothly, but that was the only thing that was not in good shape in my life. There were not many problems or stresses in my life at the time I faced the issue of my advisee's grade.

Now and Then: I was facing a peculiarly troublesome time in my life, however. I was a lame duck. I was near retirement and was worrying about my place on the faculty. I felt very sensitive about losing my status and reputation. I was feeling very vulnerable about challenges to the way we had done things in the past. I was more susceptible to going into conflict at that moment than I would have been at another time.

More or Less: Even though I was vulnerable to becoming upset because of the time in my life that the problem occurred, I do not believe I was extremely distressed. I would judge myself to be moderately in conflict. My conflict was more than less and less than more. I was feeling desperate, but I still had some control. The action I was considering was desperate. I wanted to have my way, but I did not want to destroy my colleague.

The issue of student grading was not a particularly important one to me, in and of itself. It became so as I realized that my colleague's harshness stemmed from his judgment that we had been too easy on students in the past. This was an insult to me, and I became engrossed in defending our grading policies. So, I became more distressed than I normally would have become over one student's grade. On a scale of 1–10, I became distressed at about the 7 level.

In and Out: As I thought back over the entire incident, I had to admit that there never was a time when I felt the fog of conflict lift, so to speak. I got no reprieve from my distress. I never felt I could breathe the free air of problem solving. I constantly felt ill will toward my colleague. This told me I was pretty upset and that I should treat my condition seriously. I have to admit that there was one day when he and I discussed the matter and I was able to remain calm and leave the meeting less distressed than I was when we began. But, overall, I never got enough breathing room to treat the issue as a problem; I remained in conflict.

Yes and No: So, my overall judgment was that I was, indeed, in a conflict state of mind and that I needed to follow Jesus' advice to stay in my closet until I reduced my distress. I needed to work first on my desperate sense that my self-esteem was under threat before I attempted to work with my colleague and try to reach a solution to our differences.

What can be done after we use these tools of self-examination and conclude, as I did, that we need to reduce the conflict within? As a Christian, that question has only one answer. We need to pray for "the peace of God, which passeth all understanding" (Phil. 4:7) and remain confident that the promise in Isaiah 26:3 is just as true for each of us as it has been for God's people throughout the ages. Isaiah proclaims, "Thou wilt keep him in perfect peace, whose mind is stayed on thee."

I needed peace, and God gave it to me. When we are in conflict, our desperate feelings of anxiety need to be quieted down and reduced. We Christians know that we can depend on God to do that for us. When we put our trust in Him, we can know for sure that "All is well with my soul," as the old black spiritual attests.

I conclude this chapter with a case upon which you can practice your skills of self-examination. The case is called "The

Little Drummer Boy." Take the role of the pastor in this situation and, using the five tools I have given you, decide whether or not he is in conflict. Decide whether he needs to get the "beam" out of his own eye before he deals with the "motes" in the eyes of those with whom he has a problem.

▼

LITTLE DRUMMER BOY

At about 7:45 P.M. someone was knocking at the door. It was the Nelsons' next-door neighbor. The neighbor had been disturbed by the noise the Nelsons's son, Roy, made playing his drums. She was very irritated and demanded that he stop immediately.

Thomas Nelson, Roy's father, was not home at the time. He was the pastor of First A.M.E. Zion Church and did not return from a meeting of the Men's Fellowship until 10:30 P.M. His wife told him of the incident when he came home.

Pastor Nelson did not like criticism. He took pride in having good relations with his neighbors. What had happened was embarrassing and frustrating. He also had feelings about his son. While he did not want his son to offend the neighbors, he knew that Roy was going through a tough time and that playing the drums was one way he could let off tension.

The following morning the Nelsons discussed the problem at breakfast. Several alternatives were considered, but no decisions were made.

Two days later Thomas came home for supper after a hard day of work at the church. He walked through the hall to his office and into the master bedroom at the back of the house. To his amazement he discovered that the furniture had been changed, and Roy's drums were set up where his dresser used to be.

Thomas turned around and stormed into the kitchen. "What's going on here?" he demanded. "Roy's bed and drums are in our room. Where is our furniture?" "We exchanged bedrooms with Roy so he could play his drums without disturbing the neighbors," his wife replied as she continued preparing supper. "No! No! No!" Thomas shouted. "You can't just decide to do that. Why wasn't I consulted?" Thomas rushed back to his study and sat silently at his desk.

Background

Thomas Nelson had been the pastor of First A.M.E. Zion church in Frankfort, Kentucky, for five years when this incident took place.

He was a hard worker and a good preacher. The church had grown significantly under his leadership. However, this growth was not without its price. Reverend Nelson typically worked sixty hours a week. He was fifty-nine years old and his doctor had told him that he had high blood pressure and needed to slow down. He was also trying to lose weight but having little success in doing it.

Roy, the Nelsons' youngest son, was unemployed and feeling frustrated that he did not know what he wanted to do with his life. He had quit college after his freshman year and had been unable to find work for the last six months. Interest in drums and in bands provided focus, relief, and relaxation. He was a good musician and thought that he might like to join a band.

The Nelsons had been good parents. Their other children were married and had families of their own. They were worried about Roy and sorry that he had not found himself. In addition, they were tired of childrearing and, although they were caring and supportive of Roy, they were eager for him to make a life of his own.

The neighbor who complained was an elderly woman who lived with her unmarried adult daughter. Relationships between the two households had usually been amiable although the neighbor's dog had gotten loose one day and dug up the Nelsons' garden. The Nelsons had taken over some food when the neighbor had the flu a year or so ago. The neighbor did not go to the Nelsons' church.

Reverend Nelson had always put much emphasis on having a good reputation with the neighbors. As the children were growing up, whenever complaints came he would acquiesce and adjust the children's behavior to settle the problem. However, as he thought over Roy's drum playing, he wondered if the neighbor's complaints were not overkill. After all, 7:45 P.M. is not late in the evening, and Roy had only been playing for ten minutes when she came over and complained.

Without Thomas's knowledge, his wife and Roy decided to solve the problem themselves. They thought Thomas would appreciate what they decided to do. They spent almost half a day moving Roy's furniture to the back bedroom, which had been the master bedroom. Then they moved Thomas and his wife's furniture to the front bedroom. It was *fait accompli* when Thomas came home from work.

Predicament

As Thomas sat at his desk in his home study he could hear his wife still stirring around in the kitchen. "Doesn't she know how angry and hurt I am?" he mused. "Of course, we talked about solving Roy's problem by exchanging bedrooms; but I hadn't made up my mind to do it. They did it without consulting me. This is like the last straw! Things are not going well with me. I'm tired of giving in to neighbors, to the church, to the family, to my blood pressure, to my weight, to. . . ."

▼

CHAPTER SIX

Conflict reduction calls for analysis and action

▼

For learning about wisdom and instruction,
for understanding words of insight,
for gaining instruction in wise dealing,
righteousness, justice, and equity . . .
Let the wise also hear and gain in learn ing,
and the discerning acquire a skill.
— Proverbs 1:2–3, 5 (NRSV)

Old dogs *can* learn new tricks.
— old saying (revised)

▼

I owe Harold Myhand a debt. He taught me that things are not always as easy as they seem. I was never much of an athlete, but one thing I always thought I could do was hit a softball. Baseballs, no! Softballs, yes! After all, a softball was so big it would be hard to miss—even by a nonathlete like myself. Then I met Harold.

Harold was an underhand, fastball pitcher. He went to my church and showed off his prowess at one of our picnics. He wound up, stepped forward, swung his arm around in windmill fashion and fired the softball in my direction. The ball whizzed by and did a dance as it sailed across the plate. I chopped at one or two pitches in desperation. At other times, the ball was safe in the catcher's mitt before I realized it had left Harold's fingers. I never came close to hitting the nine balls pitched to me in my three times at bat. What I thought would be easy proved to be difficult. Things are not always as they seem or as we expect them to be. I learned to respect fast softball pitching.

Sometimes Christians are like that. They think conflict reduction is easier than it is. With good intentions and Christlike optimism they rush in and stand up to bat, confident that they can hit conflict reduction home runs. Since my picnic experience I have never overestimated my batting skill again. Nor will Christians who have rushed into conflict and struck out ever overestimate their skills again. It is easy to underestimate the difficulty of hitting softballs and reducing conflict.

Unfortunately, such experiences can cause some Christians to shy away from even trying to reduce conflict—in themselves, or in other people. They avoid conflict like it was a hot stove on which they had burned their fingers.

Becoming pessimistic may be human, but it is not Christian. We are called to "bear one another's burdens" (Gal. 6:2, NRSV). One way to do this is to help others reduce the conflict feelings they are experiencing.

Being realistic in conflict reduction means taking the time to analyze the situation and to make a plan of action. The skills of Analysis and Action are the subject of this chapter. If helping someone in conflict is important, it is worth taking the time to learn how to do it. What is needed are persons who are willing to put their minds into acquiring the skills to analyze the situation and to work out a plan of action designed to help persons in distress regain enough self-esteem to return to the stress of problem solving. The quote from Proverbs with which this chapter began implies that "old dogs can learn new tricks."

The WDCCSW Model
Would Dogs Call Cats Soft Woolies?

Whether:
Decide whether someone is or is not in conflict.
▼
Did:
Put down on paper what actually happened—
event by event.
▼
Could:
Reflect upon what could have been done to prevent
persons from going into conflict.
▼
Can:
Begin to form a plan of action.
▼
Should:
Evaluate the "Can" list—which of those courses of action
should be implemented?
▼
Will:
Bring conflict reduction all together
into a detailed plan of action.
▼

A six-point method of analysis and action for helping some-one come out of conflict is called the WDCCSW Model. In this acronym; the letters stand for Whether (W), Did (D), Could (C), Can (C), Should (S), and Will (W). Hopefully, you will memorize the steps and practice the model before you try it. The memory crutch I have found helpful in recalling these steps is the nonsense question "Would Dogs Call Cats Soft Woolies?" (WDCCSW).

In preparation for reading the rest of this chapter, spread out seven sheets of paper on your desk or kitchen table. Label each one of these with the six headings of the WDCCSW Model. Put two papers under the last heading, Will (W). I'll show you later why you need these two sheets of paper.

WHETHER (W)

Making a judgment of Whether someone is "in conflict" or "not in conflict" is the first step in the WDCCSW Model for conflict reduction. With your eyes shut, think of some situation in which someone was *truly* upset; feeling extremely anxious about threats to his or her self-esteem. Ideally, think of a situation where you were not part of the problem that caused someone to go into conflict.

Recall the distinctions I made in chapter 3 on the "colors" of conflict. Look back at the chart and try to think of the kind of situation where another person was in conflict, but not over you; and where you were not in conflict yourself (the blue square). Remember, these are the easiest types of conflict situations in which you can be a helper. One last caution: think of a situation in the past, not in the present. Later on you can use the WDCCSW with some actual conflict in the present, but it will be better if you have some practice on past situations that can no longer be changed.

 Put the book down and follow the instructions.

Thinking about that situation, write down on the Whether sheet a one- or two-sentence description of the event. The following examples show the format that should be used. Identify the person and state the problem over which they went into conflict.

Example 1: "Grace went into conflict over the arrest of her son, who had charged purchases on a credit card he found on the sidewalk."

Example 2: "Horace went into conflict over not getting the job he wanted because the person they hired had less qualifications than he did."

Example 3: "José, chair of the board of deacons, went into conflict over the board's decision not to support his plan to set up a new ministry to the homeless."

Example 4: "Sharon went into conflict over learning that a woman at the annual company picnic criticized Sharon's work on the annual report."

Example 5: "Mary went into conflict when she learned that her husband had been unfaithful to her."

Take a good look at these statements. First, note that each of them makes a judgment. They reflect the fact that somebody has judged another person to have passed over the line from problem solving into conflict. It is an either/or decision.

In your case, I asked you to make a decision that this had happened. In *your opinion,* the person you have in mind was no longer just experiencing "stress," she or he was in *distress.* Now, this person was experiencing anxiety that her or his self-esteem was being gravely threatened. The person was no longer "problem solving," but was involved in trying to restore good feelings about herself or himself.

You have made a judgment that, in his or her mind, this person moved from one state of mind to another. And because of this decision you have made, you have decided to help this person in a different way than you would have had you decided they were still just "under stress."

Second, note that all the statements contain the word *over*. This word, *over*, is the way the Whether statement acknowledges that there are real-life stress situations that persons must face. These real-life issues are important, but they are not "conflicts." They are "problems." People go into conflict *over* problems; but every problem is not experienced as conflict. Remember that conflicts are states of mind inside the person. Conflict is not outside the person in the stress situation.

This understanding, that the stress situation is not the conflict, is going to be very important when we move on to the other WDCCSW steps. Often you can solve the problem, but the individual will remain in conflict. The job of the Helper is to help *reduce the conflict first* and, maybe, help the person solve the problem at a later time. Solving problems *follows* conflict reduction; it does not precede it.

So, look again at what you wrote down under the Whether (W) page. Make sure you stated it in the way that clearly reflects your awareness that you made a judgment that someone had gone into conflict over a problem situation they were facing.

 Put the book down and follow the instructions.

Once you have refined your Whether statement, indicate whether the problem should be classified as a Way, a Means, or an End issue.

Classifying Your Whether Statement:

1. A Way Problem: A difference of opinion about "how" something is to be done.

2. A Means Problem: A difference of opinion about "which" kinds of materials and resources should be used.

3. An End Problem: A difference of opinion about "what" is to be done.

Elaborate on your one- or two-sentence statement. What did you see in this person's behavior that was a clue to his or her distressful feelings? Add a few thoughts that come to mind when

you finish the sentence, "I saw distress in the way he or she. . . ."
A few illustrations of how you might finish such a sentence are:

> got red in the face;
> wept uncontrollably;
> stormed out of the room;
> locked him/herself in his/her room;
> began to perspire profusely;
> could not stop shaking;
> became silent;
> began to fight;
> started to wring his/her hands;
> shouted and threatened to hurt somebody;
> could not sit still;
> got upset and vomited;
> complained of a migraine headache;
> went to bed and slept twenty-four hours;
> broke furniture;
> tore her/his clothes;
> threatened to use a gun.

These are the kinds of behaviors that would fit the definition
of "drastic behaviors based on desperate feelings." They are
unusual, atypical, out-of-the-ordinary for most people. They are
not the sorts of things that people do in "polite society." They are
the clues we often use to make the judgment that a persons is
very, very upset. Listing these observations confirms the judgment you made that someone is in conflict. This Whether step is
the basic decision that has to be made before anything else can
be done by a Helper in conflict reduction.

 Put the book down and follow the instructions.

DID (D)

This step in the WDCCSW model forces Helpers to put down
on paper what actually happened—event by event. In this step,

the Helper makes a list of the incidents that led up to the person's going from the stress of problem solving to the distress of conflict. Helpers should think of themselves as witnesses who have been instructed by a judge to "tell us exactly what you saw."

Below is an illustration of what might be written down about the example I gave of a woman named Grace whose son was arrested for charging purchases on a credit card he found on the sidewalk. I have numbered the incidents that led up to and followed her going into conflict over her son's behavior.

1. Grace is the mother of two sons; one ten and the other eighteen years old.

2. Grace's husband divorced her last year.

3. Grace's older son did not make good grades in school.

4. Grace said she was worried about how her sons were reacting to the divorce.

5. Grace's older son could not find a summer job.

6. Grace and her older son argued over what she thought was his laziness.

7. Grace's son found a credit card on the sidewalk.

8. Grace told her son to turn the card in to the police; he did not do it.

9. Grace's son bought some things with the credit card; the total he charged was $460.

10. Grace's son then turned in the card to the police and told his mother he had done so.

11. Grace got a call at work from the police, saying they thought her son had used the card.

12. That night, Grace asked her son about the police call; he denied he had used the card to make purchases.

13. A few days later, Grace got a call at work from her son; he had been arrested and was in jail.

14. Grace called her friend and cried uncontrollably.

15. Grace went to court with her son.

16. Grace's son was sentenced to probation.

17. Grace stopped going to church.

18. Grace began to oversleep and be late for work.

This list of eighteen events is the story seen from the eyes of a Helper who wants to see what can be done to reduce Grace's conflict. These events may not tell the entire story. There is probably much more that was happening. However, the Helper did not observe them and, thus, could not know them. Such a list is the truth as seen from an outsider's viewpoint—nothing more, nothing less. This list provides a way to pinpoint the time when a person goes from stress to distress, from the viewpoint of someone who is trying to be a Helper.

Try your hand at this exercise. Look over my list of Grace's situation. Put a check where, in your best judgment, Grace seemed to go into conflict. What number did you check? I would have checked number fourteen because it was at that point that Grace started behaving in an unusual manner. She was not the sort of woman who usually cried uncontrollably—as if she felt things were completely out of hand.

Take a moment to make a list of the incidents that led to the situation that you described in the Whether step. On your Did sheet write the facts that you know about that led up to and followed the time the person went into conflict. Number these facts just as I did. Put a check beside the event during which you think the person went from stress to distress.

 Put the book down and follow the instructions.

What do you have so far in the Whether (W) and the Did (D) steps? You have identified a person you think was in conflict. You have noted the problem over which they went into conflict and typed it as an issue of Ways, Means, or Ends. Further, you have noted the unusual behaviors you observed that indicated the individual was acting in a drastic manner. These were the components of the Whether step in conflict reduction.

Then, you have made a list of the events that led up to and followed the time when the person passed over from the stress of problem solving to the distress of conflict. You have noted the point in time when this happened. These are the components of the Did step in conflict reduction.

These two steps will help you get a clearer picture of the conflict process. Taking these steps forces the Helper to be as objective as possible. This is particularly important if one was a part of the situation over which the other person went into conflict.

I asked you to choose a situation where you were not involved, but this is not always the case. In the most difficult situations, the individual would have gone into conflict *over* something done by the person who is trying to help. In such cases, the first step Helpers should take is to get out of conflict themselves. This was emphasized in the chapters on the colors of conflict (3) and on conflict reduction (4). You can not be a good Helper while you are in conflict yourself. After getting yourself out of conflict, the second step is to deal with the feelings the other person is having.

COULD (C)

This third step in the WDCCSW conflict reduction model is very important. In the Could step, Helpers reflect upon what they could have done to prevent persons from going into conflict. We must never forget how desperate people feel when they are in distress. It doesn't take much memory for most of us to remember that, when we were in conflict, it was a terrible experience. So, it goes without saying that if something could have been done to keep us from having such an experience, we would have wanted it to be done.

Although it may sound a bit paternalistic to say that if anything could be done, it should be done, as a counselor I can tell you that this is exactly how I feel. Conflict is such a devastating experience that I, personally, am willing to run the risk of seeming to be overly protective in trying to prevent it.

Some critics of this third step think it is not necessary for another reason. They insist that what is past is past. The past cannot be relived. They contend that it would be better to spend time focusing on the present. I disagree with this point of view although I do agree that it is the present that should be our prime concern. Yet, examining the past may cause us to see some things that still could be done. In addition, there may be things that can be undone, especially if Helpers discover that they played a part in making the situations so stressful that persons became distressed.

So, take the time now to list on the Could sheet a list of things that you could have done to have kept the person in your situation from passing over the line from stress to distress. Take your time and see what actions come to your mind.

Look back over your list and see if you can identify which of the possibilities would have helped you Detect, Detain, or Deter the conflict experience.

 Put the book down and follow the instructions.

▼ Detect: the kind of actions that might have shown the other person you realized they were getting upset.

▼ Detain: the kind of actions that might have been taken to keep people from passing over the line from stress to distress.

▼ Deter: the kind of actions that might have kept someone from becoming more distressed once he *had* gone into conflict.

For example, in the Grace situation, the Helper might have detected that the stress was piling up after the divorce, when the son did not do well in school, or after Grace told her friend about her son's difficulty in finding a job. A Helper could have expressed concern to Grace and been willing to listen to her stress.

Further, in the case of Grace, the Helper might have said, "If only I had been sensitive enough to realize what Grace was going through and called her the night before the trial to see how she was doing," or "I could have gone to court with Grace and supported her when the trial occurred," or "I should have known that things were piling up for Grace. I could have gone over to have coffee with her from time to time." These were things that might have detained Grace from becoming distressed over the situation.

Keeping the conflict from becoming worse is also important. In the case of Grace, the Helper might have deterred the conflict by concluding, "I could have called Grace every night to see how she was doing after she cried like she did," or "I could have offered to take her to supper the night after the court trial," or "When Grace didn't show up for church two weeks in a row, I could have called her to listen to what she was feeling." These are examples of what could have been done to deter the conflict.

Now look back over your list and think about how your actions might have been used to Detect, Detain, or Deter the conflict in the person you are thinking about.

 Put the book down and follow the instructions.

The sole purpose of this Could step in conflict reduction is to generate ideas that still might be good to try as you move to the next step, where a plan of action is developed.

Three observations need to be made. First, when you reflect on what you could have done, you may end up with no list at all. You may not come up with anything that you could have done to detect, detain, or deter the conflict. The situation may have been entirely out of your hands. You may have come into the person's life after they had gone into conflict. This is often true. Don't criticize yourself if nothing comes to mind.

The second observation is that, while you may have a list, none of the things that could have been done can still be done.

That, too, is OK. Sometimes the past is truly the past. You have to begin with what is still possible. The only value of the list in this case is to help you identify the things that you *cannot* do.

Finally, if perchance you were part of the problem over which the person went into conflict, the kinds of things that can still be done take on a special character. If you really care about the person, as I hope you would, the list may make it clear that you need to back down on what you did to provoke the distress no matter how strongly you believe in what you did. As I stated in the last chapter, persons are more important than issues. You may even need to ask for forgiveness. Certainly, you will need to apologize.

CAN (C)

The Can step is the point at which Helpers begin to move from Analysis to Action. The Can step is the point at which a plan of Action begins to take form. On the basis of what you know from the Whether, Did, and Could steps, Helpers now consider what *can* be done to help reduce distress and assist persons in moving back across the line from distress to the stress of problem solving.

Act as if the time is the present and you still have the opportunity to help, even if the situation in this exercise happened a long time ago. Remember, your goal is to be of help in restoring your friend's self-esteem so that he or she will feel good enough about him or herself to cease acting desperately and begin to act rationally.

For Helpers, thinking about what can be done is best undertaken by leaning back, looking up at the ceiling, and letting the mind begin to wander—wherever it wants to go! This is what is meant by "brainstorming." Helpers should put their minds into neutral gear and allow any and all possibilities to float up to the surface of their minds.

On the Can sheet try your skill at doing this. Write down any and all ideas you can think of, anything that might make your friend feel better.

It sometimes helps to loosen up your thinking by being humorous or outlandish. This Can list does not commit you to doing any of these things. It's just a list. In the Should and Will steps that follow, you have a chance to select the best ideas on the list. Right now, just write down whatever idea comes to mind—no matter how crazy, unreasonable, or funny it might be.

Researchers have found that giving yourself permission to write down any and all thoughts in this way often results in very creative ideas coming to mind.

To illustrate what I mean, I will brainstorm a list of what I might do in the Grace situation. I will begin by examining my Could options to see if there are any that would still be possibilities. Then, I will add what new ideas have come to my mind.

1. I could encourage Grace to take a week's vacation.

2. I could take Grace out to supper and a movie.

3. I could suggest that Grace order her son to leave.

4. I could call Grace's pastor and suggest he visit her.

5. I could enroll Grace in the dial-a-date program.

6. I could offer to pay Grace's son's fine.

7. I could ask Grace if I could pray with her.

8. I could buy Grace a gun so she could shoot the judge.

9. I could arrange for Grace to see a lawyer.

10. I could invite Grace to a church fellowship meeting.

11. I could encourage Grace to confront her son with her feelings.

12. I could ask Grace to go with me on a weekend trip.

13. I could buy Grace a new dress.

14. I could pray for Grace.

15. I could ask Grace to study the Bible with me.

16. I could help Grace plant a garden.

17. I could paint a sign for Grace's door which said "Son for Sale."

18. I could reassure Grace that I was her friend whatever happened.

19. I could suggest that Grace and her son go for counseling.

20. I could buy Grace some pep pills.

21. I could shoot Grace's son.

22. I could find Grace a new husband.

23. I could help Grace lock up her son and never let him out.

24. I could go for coffee with Grace.

As you can see, there were some things on the Could (C) list that are still possibilities. There are things I could have done that I still can do. This proves the value of my reflecting on what I could have done to detect, detain, and deter Grace from going into conflict.

Also note that not all the Could ideas are still do-able. I just ignored them without any further thought. The past is the past, and those opportunities are no more. However, by brainstorming I came up with a number of novel and creative new ideas. My list is the combination of the old and the new.

Now it's your turn. After looking over your Could options and brainstorming new ideas, make a list on the Can sheet of ways you could help your friend reduce his/her feelings of distress.

 Put the book down and follow the instructions.

After you have made this list, go back over it and identify which of the things that could be done are Defensive, Conventional, and Transcendent alternatives (see chap. 4). Remember that each of these ways of reducing conflict works, and a combination of alternatives is probably best. By grouping your Can list into these three sections, you will be even clearer about how to proceed as we move to the Should and Will steps, where Helpers decide on actual plans of action.

SHOULD (S)

In the Should step we evaluate the Can list. Making a list did not commit you to doing anything. The list only provided you with a set of options that will need to be evaluated. The list does provide the basic ingredients of a plan of action, however. The next task is to combine the ingredients in this conflict reduction recipe and bake a cake that can be eaten, to coin a phrase.

The Can list has to be evaluated on the basis of Style, Function, and Value. Only those actions that meet all three criteria should be included in the final plan. Let me explain these three ways to evaluate the Can list of alternatives.

Style means just what it says—"*my* style." The first question a Helper should ask is, "Could I do it?" or "Is it my style?" Your answer might be, It might be a good idea, but it just wouldn't be possible for me to do it; it just wouldn't be *me!* This may sound crazy, but Helpers need to be honest with themselves. We all have our unique quirks, things we can and cannot do, our styles. The list needs to be evaluated on whether a given Helper personally could do or could not do it.

Function means, "Would doing this work?" "Would it function to help reduce the distress feelings?" This is an important pragmatic question. Only those things that you think would actually work with the Person who is in conflict should be included in the final plan.

Value means, "Is this thing a *good* thing to do?" or "Would it be a thing that God would approve of?" Here Helpers apply the standard of goodness. After spending all this energy in analysis, Helpers should only want a final plan that includes behaviors that have value. Evaluating the options in terms of their value, of ideals, is important—especially for Christian Helpers.

Ideally, only those ideas that are rated yes in all three ways should end up being a part of the final plan that will be decided upon in the Will (W) step to follow.

I have evaluated my list to show how this might be done. Note that I used a plus sign (+) to stand for yes and a minus sign (-) to stand for no as I evaluated of each option. The first plus or minus answers the question "Could I really do it?" The second plus or minus answers the question "Would it work?" The third plus or minus answers the question "Is it a good thing to do?"

1. I could encourage Grace to take a week's vacation. +,+,+

2. I could take Grace out to supper and a movie. +,+,+

3. I could suggest that Grace order her son to leave. -,+,-

4. I could call Grace's pastor and suggest he visit her. +,+,+

5. I could enroll Grace in the dial-a-date program. -,-,+

6. I could offer to pay Grace's son's fine. -,+,+

7. I could ask Grace if I could pray with her. +,+,+

8. I could buy Grace a gun so she could shoot the judge. -,-,-

9. I could arrange for Grace to see a lawyer. +,+,+

10. I could invite Grace to a church fellowship meeting. +,+,+

11. I could encourage Grace to confront her son with her feelings. +,+,+

12. I could ask Grace to go with me on a weekend trip. -,+,+

13. I could buy Grace a new dress. +,-,-

14. I could pray for Grace. +,+,+

15. I could ask Grace to study the Bible with me. -,+,+

16. I could help Grace plant a garden. -,-,+

17. I could paint a sign for Grace's door which said "Son for Sale." -,+,-

18. I could reassure Grace that I was her friend whatever happened. +,+,+

19. I could suggest that Grace and her son go for counseling. +,+,+

20. I could buy Grace some pep pills. +,-,+

21. I could shoot Grace's son. -,-,-

22. I could help Grace find a new husband. -,+,+

23. I could help Grace lock up her son and never let him out. -,+,-

24. I could go for coffee with Grace. +,+,+

Do these pluses and minuses make sense? You might not agree with me because the judgments about what *I* would do may not be what *You* would do in this situation. But, I can assure you that behind each judgment is a personal reflection that I could justify if we sat down and talked with each other. You probably would make different judgments because we are all unique. That is the secret of this process.

It is you, the individual Helper, who makes the judgments because it is you, the individual Helper, who must carry out the plan. No plan is absolutely perfect. Each one has strengths and weaknesses. Each plan may or may not succeed in conflict reduction. But each plan has a greater chance of reducing conflict if it has been well thought out by the one who will undertake it.

Take the time now to look back over the list that you have made and make judgments about each of the options you have written. Decide whether it is your style, whether it will work, and whether it is a good thing to do.

 Put the book down and follow the instructions.

WILL (W)

The Will step in conflict reduction is the place where it all comes together in a detailed plan of action. It is the time when the evaluations of the Can options in the Should step are put into an actual schedule of actions that are to be undertaken. The way to start is for the Helper to identify all those actions which were rated by at least two pluses (+,+) in the Should step. This can be done best by taking a yellow highlighter and marking through each option that has two pluses by its side. For example, in my list of Grace options I would highlight the following actions:

1. I could encourage Grace to take a week's vacation. +,+,+

2. I could take Grace out to supper and a movie. +,+,+

4. I could call Grace's pastor and suggest he visit her. +,+,+

6. I could offer to pay Grace's son's fine. -,+,+

7. I could ask Grace if I could pray with her. +,+,+

9. I could arrange for Grace to see a lawyer. +,+,+

10. I could invite Grace to a church fellowship meeting. +,+,+

11. I could encourage Grace to confront her son with her feelings. +,+,+

12. I could ask Grace to go with me on a weekend trip. -,+,+

14. I could pray for Grace. +,+,+

15. I could ask Grace to study the Bible with me. -,+,+

18. I could reassure Grace that I was her friend whatever happened. +,+,+

19. I could suggest that Grace and her son go for counseling. +,+,+

20. I could buy Grace some pep pills. +,-,+

22. I could help Grace find a new husband. -,+,+

24. I could go for coffee with Grace. +,+,+

These options become the actions I would take as a Helper to Grace. The only thing that remains for me to do is to decide which I will do first, which second, which third, etc. Before we go on, look at your list and highlight those items that you have rated with two or three pluses.

 Put the book down and follow the instructions.

At last we are ready to make our plans of action. We are ready to decide what we will do to help someone reduce their conflict.

I asked you to put Will on two sheets of paper. On one we will list things we will do *immediately,* and on the other we will list things we will do over the next month or two. Write Now on one of the Will sheets and Future on the other. Some actions will appear on both sheets, some on only one. Some things will be good to do only once, some should be done again and again.

It is important not to forget that the goal of conflict reduction is to reduce feelings. We are not problem solving. The aim is to reduce the distressed feelings to the point where persons can be calm enough to solve problems without their emotions getting in the way. Feelings are much more complex than ideas, so the reason for having a Now and a Future plan is that feelings may take a long time to change.

Persons may feel better very soon with our Now plan of action only to discover that their old feelings of distress return at some time in the future. That is why Helpers need a long-term plan of action. Feelings often return, and the helping process will take time. It is not as easy to reduce conflict as it is to help solve problems.

One final caution is needed before I illustrate how I might design a Now and a Future plan of action to help Grace. There is a saying my mother used to repeat when things did not go as she had planned: "The best laid plans of mice and men often go astray." Our best predictions of what will help in conflict reduction often fail. So when making a plan of action, it is best to have a substitute idea in mind in case the first option fails to help the person come back from distress to stress. We hope our plan works, but it may not.

Furthermore, those we are trying to help may not be honest with us. Nobody likes to admit they are feeling distressed. People might like to please us. They may say they are feeling better only to realize that they are still upset sometime later. All of this is to say that we can only make guesses of what is going on inside another person. But we should have an alternative idea in mind if we think that what we did failed.

So, my Now and my Future plans of action to reduce Grace's feelings of distress can be seen in the diagrams on the following pages. Note that they are diagramed in a Decision Tree format

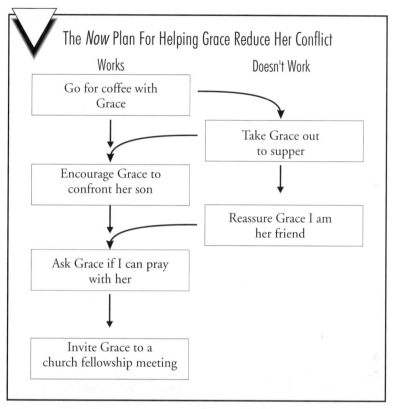

The *Now* Plan For Helping Grace Reduce Her Conflict

Note: The goal is to reduce the conflict inside Grace so that she can return to problem solving. The model illustrated here takes into account that your effort does not always work. If it does not reduce the conflict, then another attempt is made, etc. etc.

that takes into account the possibility that things don't always work out as planned. It acknowledges the truth of the illustration with which this chapter began: "Things are not as easy as they seem." But what does result from this type of planning is that one has a plan of action that has the possibility, if not the probability, of working.

As you can see, there are no guarantees that either the Now or the Future plans will work. There is the probability that Grace would respond positively to the support of the Helper, and there

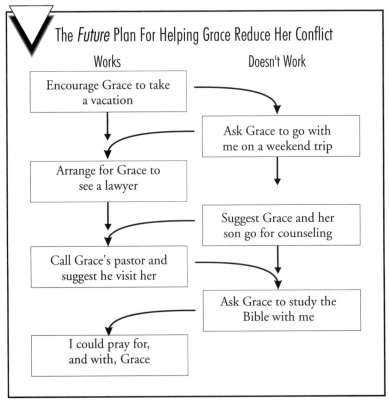

The *Future* Plan For Helping Grace Reduce Her Conflict

Works	Doesn't Work
Encourage Grace to take a vacation	Ask Grace to go with me on a weekend trip
Arrange for Grace to see a lawyer	Suggest Grace and her son go for counseling
Call Grace's pastor and suggest he visit her	Ask Grace to study the Bible with me
I could pray for, and with, Grace	

Note: The reason for a Future plan is that conflict feelings have a habit of lingering and returning. Reducing the conflict and returning to problem solving requires long-term effort. The Future plan takes this into account.

is the probability that she would experience a new-found strength to face her problems. The regaining of her self-esteem is the desired outcome. Note that the problem Grace has with her son did not go away. Hopefully, she will have the inner strength to handle the situation.

Take the time to complete the Will task on your own case. Using the options you have identified as having two or more pluses, sketch out a Now and Future plan of action for your friend who was in conflict. Make sure you keep in mind what you would do if your original plan failed.

Put the book down and follow the instructions.

As you look over what you have done, you may feel exhausted. The WDCCSW model may seem too complicated to really work. I can assure that this is not so. Conflict reduction is much more complicated than problem solving, and all the effort you put into working this model will pay off in the end.

▼

CHAPTER SEVEN

Conflicts can be prevented

▼

A stitch in time saves nine.
— old saying

▼

Conflicts can be prevented. A "stitch" in time can save "nine." A tear in the fabric does not have to become a top-to-bottom rip in the cloth. Regular preventive maintenance can keep material strong. Any good seamstress knows this. The same is true for conflict.

Conflicts are like termites, which can cause wooden floors to give way unexpectedly—*except* in those buildings where exterminators regularly check beneath the floor and take steps to prevent termites from ever getting a hold.

I am confident that conflict can be prevented. We do not have to wait until conflict comes to do something about it. As in Aesop's famous fable of the grasshopper and the squirrel, it is possible for us to act like squirrels and lay up for ourselves the "nuts" of conflict prevention—before winter comes. Unlike the grasshopper, we do not have to lounge lazily against our oak trees fantasizing that the season will never change or, if it does, pretending that we could have done nothing to prepare for it.

Yes, conflict can be anticipated and prevented. Conflict may be inevitable, but it is not necessary; it doesn't have to happen, but it probably will. Conflict is not written in stone, even though it seems to occur with a haunting frequency. Anticipation of inevitable conflict has the potential of preventing it with an equally amazing frequency.

Several years ago I conducted a conflict management workshop for a group of Roman Catholic nuns in Erie, Pennsylvania. They had a book listing all the goals of their order. These ideals read like the statements that are often written on church stationery, found in brochures in pew racks, or seen emblazoned on banners at the front of sanctuaries. These Benedictine sisters stated that they intended "to be a fellowship where love abides," "to be servants of Christ for the world," and "to pray for the salvation of all the world."

Following this page stating their goals and ideals was a section they called "Rules." These "rules" included a set of statements about the guidelines they would use in living together. They detailed how they intended to handle problems when they arose. They described the procedures they would follow in making decisions. They listed how they would solve differences and what they would do in times of crisis. Their leader and the writer of this list, Sister Joan Chichester—a nationally known leader—had prefaced this list of rules with this statement, "We have these rules so that we will not kill each other."

When I read her statement, I laughed out loud. I thought it was funny that a group would have a book that stated in such flowery language their unselfish goals, their high ideals, and their loving intentions, yet follow these with a set of rules so that they would not KILL each other! *Amazing,* I said to myself, *What a contradiction!*

Then I stopped and thought. *No, this is not a contradiction; it is stark realism. Such a statement is being brutally honest; it's absolutely truthful.* I said to myself, *These nuns are right; people don't have to kill each other—although there is always the possibility that they will, even under the best conditions. Murder can be prevented. Sister Joan is absolutely correct,* I mused. *People need rules that will keep them from killing each other—even in such groups as churches and among such persons as Christians who are trying to live together in peace and love.* And what is true about possible conflict among Benedictine sisters is true for us, among our families, our committees, our friends, our coworkers, and our world.

Furthermore, I have decided that what was good for the Benedictine Sisters of Erie can provide a model for the rest of us. We can have agreed-upon ways for preventing conflict; we can have rules that keep us from killing each other; we can adopt rules for living together that assure each of us a chance to be heard when frustrations arise.

Rules work! I trust them! I am confident that Christians can settle their differences without waging war. It is possible. In fact, it is probable, *if* people adopt "conflict prevention" rules and follow them. As the maxim states, conflict can be prevented if we "plan our work, then work our plan." Like healthy marital partners, termite exterminators, and dutiful seamstresses, we can prevent the worst from happening if we expend some effort in conflict prevention.

When to Make the Rules

In making rules for conflict prevention, one caution is necessary: "Don't Wait!" Rules won't work if they are not preset. The grasshopper in Aesop's fable learned this the hard way. He came begging at the squirrel's door when winter came, but it was too late. Agreeing on rules for handling frustrating problems after crises arise is like locking your garage door after someone has stolen your car. It is too late. Your car is gone.

When I counsel couples about to be married, I always say, "You should adopt some rules for preventing conflict—right now at the beginning of your marriage." Unfortunately, I have to work hard to convince them because they are so filled with love for each other that they find it hard to think that a day might come when they would argue with each other. I am convinced, however, if I were able to go back and interview all of the couples I have married, I would find two things: one, I would find that every one of them has had times of conflict; and, two, that those couples who have the best marriages would be those who listened to me and took the time early in their relationship to adopt some conflict prevention rules.

Unlike hurricanes, conflicts are not calmest at the center of the storm. There is a reason for this. When folk pass over the line from stress to distress, from problem solving into conflict, they give in to their feelings. In conflict, it is emotion—not reason—that controls behavior.

Rules are based on reason and logic; trying to reduce conflict is not. It is very difficult, although not impossible, for people in conflict to be reasonable. Think of how often you have said to somebody in conflict, "Be reasonable!" It is highly improbable that persons in conflict will suddenly stop their desperate feelings to sit down and help design some rules that would have prevented their anxiety in the first place!

The only hope is if the rules have been *agreed upon ahead of time,* when everybody is getting along well with each other and before conflict arises. If everybody knows the rules and agrees to them, there is great likelihood that when a situation looks like it may turn into a conflict, they will follow the rules. Someone can say, "Hey, let's stop and think. We all agreed to do such-and-such when situations like this arose. Let's go back and follow our rules."

For example, Jesus gave Christians one rule to follow when we feel that we have been wronged and are in danger of going into conflict. Matthew 18:15 states, "If thy brother shall trespass against thee, go and tell him his fault between thee and him alone: if he shall hear thee, thou hast gained thy brother."

As a beginning step, we need to lift up this guideline, state it often to one another. We need to remind ourselves of this in times of peaceful interaction with each other. We need to state it often publicly. We need to bring it to mind again and again. Only when we have done this will it be possible for us to call each other to follow it when extreme stress arises. This admonition follows the well-tested rule, "Settle a thing at the lowest level possible." In other words, don't let a brush fire become a forest fire; calm yourself and settle the matter as simply as you can.

That is exactly what the Christian Conciliation Service does. The Christian Conciliation Service is a group of lawyers that offers help to Christians who are about to sue each other in court. If lawyers on both sides of the controversy find out that their clients are Christians, they encourage them to live up to Jesus' admonition in Matthew 18:25. They remind them that this is a "rule" Christians have agreed they would follow if, and when, they become estranged from each other. The lawyers challenge the plaintiff and defendant to live up to this ideal and follow the rule that Jesus gave to His followers.

In many situations they have helped Christians resolve their differences without going to court, without going into conflict with each other, and without getting into a win-lose battle. The Christian Conciliation Service has helped Christians "gain brothers" instead of remaining "enemies" because the combatants followed a rule that they agreed to follow, a rule that was set long before their relationship broke down.

In practically none of these cases would the "new" brothers have been willing to sit down and decide on a "Christian" rule for talking with one another *after* the court suit had been filed. When the matter was filed with the court, it would have been too late. The rule had to exist *before* the controversy, before the parties went into conflict with each other. Then, and only then, could the Christian Conciliation Service lawyers call upon them to obey the rule.

Unfortunately, although the Bible often encourages us to live in peace with one another (Mark 9:50; 2 Cor. 13:11; 1 Thess. 5:13), this Matthew 18:15 rule is one of very few guidelines for making it happen. Conflict prevention, which can lead to peace, is a skill that requires us to use our best thinking ahead of time. We need to be *thinking* Christians.

Hopefully, the "rules" we come up with in our various relationships will support and honor the way Christ would have us behave. Maybe we can even be so bold as to think that Christ is guiding us through His Holy Spirit as we do our thinking and as we state our rules. Personally, I am convinced that one of the prime locations of the image of God in us is in the frontal lobe of our brains, where most of our good rational thinking occurs.

Contrary to the old adage, "If it ain't broke, don't fix it," the intent of my recommendation to set rules for interacting *before* conflict arises is "Fix it long before it breaks!" Let's do some thinking together, therefore, about the type of rules that could help prevent conflict from arising.

Rule 1: Encourage Differences of Opinion

One thing that is easy to forget is that differences of opinion are good, not bad. Earlier, I contended that God intends that people take stands, have opinions, and look at things from

different viewpoints. God told Adam and Eve to "have dominion" *before* they committed sin and *before* He banished them from
the Garden of Eden. This should tell us that we, like Adam and
Eve, are put here to do something with our lives, to use our minds,
and to enter into life with enthusiasm and gusto.

To have dominion means to enter into the discussion, to
evaluate situations, make judgments, have opinions, have a point
of view, and take a stand. Human beings are supposed to be
unique. That is what it means to be made in the image of God.
We are new creations (2 Cor. 5:17); we are to be cocreators with
Him; we are meant by God to use our minds; to think and have
ideas; to evaluate, make judgments, and express our opinions.

I repeat this point about the unique importance of every
person's point of view because it is difficult sometimes for Christians to realize that this applies to them. This is especially difficult
in an environment, such as religion, where we look to pastors to
lead us and to church leaders to disciple us. Likewise, traditionally,
families have counted on husbands and fathers to make final
decisions. It is hard to think that we have a right to our opinions
in settings like these.

I'm not saying that relying on these authorities is wrong. I am
saying that the best leadership involves everyone in making
decisions; in everybody taking responsibility for what happens.
This is true in the family, in business, and in religion. Each of us
needs to take an active role in life. We were not intended to "roll
over and play dead" or be like sheep who are always willing to be
led by those above us—just because they have the power, the
prestige, or the position.

Every Christian, from the youngest to the oldest, needs to
remain involved. Real leaders know how important this is in
enlisting support for their work. The best followers are those who
feel they have played a part in the discussion of what to do. We
should be proud to have been given the power to react by God.
More often than not, people go into conflict when they think
their opinions are not respected.

Some leaders are very authoritarian. They assume that they know what is best for us; that we couldn't be as knowledgeable as they are about God's will; that we need them to make decisions for us; and that our role is to follow and not ask questions. This viewpoint about leadership needs to be resisted. We are Protestant Christians who owe a debt to Martin Luther's thesis about the "priesthood of all believers." Each of us can think; each of us can pray; each of us can read the Bible. We can ask questions; we can have opinions; we are not dumb! Leaders, as well as followers, should never forget this basic truth.

The psalmist concluded, "The highest heavens belong to the Lord, but the earth he has given to man" (115:16, NIV). And "man," in this verse, means "women," too. We are indeed "made . . . a little lower than the angels . . . crowned . . . with glory and honor" (Ps. 8:5).

Those leaders who want members to be loyal and committed followers take seriously the admonition to involve them in the decisions that are made. Where this happens, followers play their roles well and accept the leader's invitation to have an opinion. People feel dignified when they feel their opinions are important.

Being heard is probably more important than having people always agree. A friend of mine did a study of congregations and found this to be true. Where people were given the chance to express their ideas, there was far less resistance to the decisions that were made, even when things didn't go the way people wanted them to go! It is very important for leaders to realize that the opposition they sometimes experience is due to people feeling insulted because they were not consulted in the decision.

Most of us can identify with the feelings of the church members in my friend's research. We know that we are better followers when we have been included in the dialogue. We have an opinion whether we get to express it or not. We need to be honest with ourselves and acknowledge how hurt we feel when we are left out of the discussion and are simply told what to do. Not feeling heard plants the seed for the feelings that can lead us into conflict; that can push us over from stress to distress.

So the first rule of conflict prevention is to honor individuals and encourage differences. The motto might be, "It's OK to be different and it's all right to disagree." Debate is healthy and can prevent conflict, rather than cause it. As the early twentieth-century jurist, Louis D. Brandeis, claimed, "In the frank expression of conflicting opinions lies the greatest promise of wisdom." Brandeis's statement was but a restatement of the thirteenth-century philosopher Saskya Pandita, who said, "It may happen sometimes that a longer debate becomes the cause of a longer friendship."

Do you remember the saying that was popular several years ago that "Real men don't eat quiche"? Well, this rule of encouraging others to express their thoughts could lead to this saying, "Real leaders don't squelch people's opinions; real leaders like to hear what people are thinking."

If we are leaders, putting this rule into practice will be easier to *say* than to *do* for two reasons. Many of the issues Christians disagree about are based on correctly interpreting the Bible. The Bible gives us divine, not human, truth. When leaders are convinced that they know what the Bible says, they tend to think that they hold an opinion that is non-negotiable. It is not a simple matter of a difference of opinion; it is a matter of truth and falsehood—at least this is how religious leaders sometimes feel. To be asked to let people express their opinions and be open to hearing what they have to say on biblical matters is very difficult.

I understand and agree that the Bible is the final authority for Christian living. I also agree that we Christians need to take our stand in opposition to those who might think that the Bible is just an antiquated book of ancient literature or that it does not contain the Word of God for us today. I am not opposed to our asserting that our convictions are nonnegotiable when we come face to face with the secular world.

Yet, I still believe it is possible for us to adopt the "conflict prevention rule of honoring differences of opinion" among Christians—even about what the Bible says. Here is the key to my conviction: We need to keep in mind that we are all Christians who are trying to find and live by the will of God for our lives. We are not enemies. We are brothers and sisters in Christ.

If we remember this truth and make this assumption when we are discussing biblical truths, we can give everyone a chance to express an opinion. The Bible is not as easy to understand as people sometimes think. Discussion is appropriate for believers, even about what the Bible says and means.

For Christians, the differences they have about scriptural matters are usually differences in "degree" not in "kind." By this I mean that even in the worst disputes, Christians of wide differences of opinion will still believe the Bible is God's Word for us. They will disagree on how, when, and to what degree we should apply the rules of the Bible and, probably more importantly, whether we should take other facts into consideration when we make our decisions.

I certainly don't mean to gloss over important distinctions in these matters or pretend that serious differences should be ignored. But leaders should remember these are differences among Christians who are called to obey Matthew 18:15. They are differences among brothers and sisters in Christ. The disputes are not Crusade-like battles with infidels who should be exterminated at all costs. Although there may be times when Christians do, indeed, part company with each other, those times should be moments when all agree with the saying:

In some things there is unity,
In other things there is diversity,
In all things there is love.

It is also hard for some leaders to invite disagreement because there is a natural tendency for us to rationalize and defend ourselves when we are criticized. Often, when people are invited to express their opinions, they render a judgment about *what* we have done or *how* we have done something.

All of us have a "style." We do things in certain ways and with distinct finesse. No leader likes to be criticized—especially about his or her style. Although leaders know better, they fantasize that everybody will like how they do what they do. They feel that what they do is the very best thing that could have been done and that this should be appreciated by one and all. This is never true, but leaders forget it and wish it wasn't so.

Concerning parents, those leaders to which we are all exposed, Fritz Perls once said, "Parents are NEVER right!" Most of us who are parents often fantasize that we are "right" 100 percent of the time. The truth, of course, lies somewhere between "never" and "100 percent." It is painful for us leaders, be we parents, bosses, pastors, or officers, to admit that we are not always right, or that the *way* we did it might not please everybody. A committee chairman recently sought my counsel about a healing ministry being planned at her church. She was frustrated by what happened at the first meeting of the committee. Some members wanted to start the ministry the next Sunday; others wanted to make some visits to other churches to see what they were doing. She wanted the group to spend several weeks discussing the meaning of "health" and "cures." Several resisted the delay and felt that they might bog down in "talk."

As she reflected on her frustration, she had a good insight. She said, "I have to admit that as they began to disagree with my plan, I became defensive because I thought they didn't like me." What a good insight this was! She was so right about leadership. Leadership is a very vulnerable role. We often take opposition personally and begin to defend ourselves—sometimes irrationally and desperately. This makes us hesitant about asking people for their opinions. They might give them to us, and we might become defensive.

I once saw a humorous cartoon about a letter a pastor wrote to his wife after she had evaluated his sermon as less than perfect, a not uncommon feeling for church members as well as pastors' wives. On Sunday afternoon while he still felt good about the service, he began a letter to her with the words, "My dear wife, Eloise." However, on Tuesday, after he had time to think, he decided that she was being unfairly critical. So, before mailing the letter he crossed out his first beginning and began the letter with the phrase, "Now hear this, Eloise." He then wrote in the statement, "If you can't say something nice, then don't say anything at all" and ended his letter with "Your minister" instead of "Your loving husband."

Nobody likes to be criticized, and it is hard to remember that all our leadership takes place this side of heaven. It is not perfect. No matter how much we pray, we will remain sinners until we die. Whatever we do, we could have done differently or better. But it is hard to remember this and somewhat embarrassing for others to point this out. Yet, this is what this rule about giving people a chance to express themselves is all about. Leaders, as well as followers, need to remember how much importance people place on their personal opinions. The maxim might be "let people have an opinion; be open to feedback no matter how stinging it might be."

I still remember one anonymous evaluation I received at the end of a class I once taught on adult psychotherapy. He (or she) wrote, "This professor needs psychotherapy." Even though I know you can't please everybody, I still remember this remark more than all the supportive comments that were made by other students. I know how hard it is to accept negative remarks, and I am the one who writes books on the subject! Preventing conflict by encouraging people to express an opinion may be frustrating, but it is one sure way to forestall the kind of conflict feelings that lead to war. We should do it even if we do not like it.

Of course, there is one final reason why leaders are sometimes reluctant to open up every issue for discussion. That is because there are some people who have something to say every time, even when they know nothing about the matter at hand. We often see their names in "Letters to the Editor" newspaper columns at the bottom of statements on issues as varied as pet control and world peace.

In addition, there are people who get emotional about every little thing; and they sometimes incite others to become upset when there is little need. These types of people are often thought to be more trouble than they are worth. Opening up issues to free discussion invites them to "do their thing." Knowing the possibility that these individuals might become involved provokes some leaders to hold back on promising that everyone will be given the opportunity to share reactions.

An associate minister once told me a story that illustrated the ambivalence leaders sometimes have about free discussion. At a board meeting in his church one evening, there was a vigorous discussion over how much to spend on repairing the roof. Suddenly one man stood up, slapped the table in front of him hard with his hand, then shouted, "I've had enough of this! You never listen to me. I've been on this board for twenty years and you've never paid attention. I'm quitting." He stormed out of the room. The senior minister went right on with the meeting and paid no attention to the angry man. When the associate asked why, the reply was, "He's acted like that again and again; I decided not to let it bother us."

In spite of the fact that there are, indeed, some characters who will take advantage of discussions and become easily angered or volunteer their ignorance, the benefit of openness is greater than the risk of disruptions. Most persons will value the invitation to have an opinion and will not misuse it for false ends.

So, rule 1 is to make it known that everyone can have an opinion or ask questions without being chastised or put down. Being different is OK. Provide chances for feedback. This will forestall a lot of distress, and people will feel better about themselves and the rules so that wars will become far less frequent.

Rule 2: State the Method, Not Just the Principle

Rule 1 was the principle; rule 2 is the method. People need to know how their opinions will be handled. It is not enough to state, "We will give folks a chance to say what they think." People want to know "when and how" they will have that chance.

People are suspicious about promises. We all know what "idle promises" are. Every week we receive promises about prizes that could be ours in the mail. Most of the time we pay no attention and throw these promises in the waste basket, even when they have our names spelled correctly! We do not believe and place trust in leaders' promises that we will have a chance to state our opinion. Leaders should make sure these suspicions never get started.

So, rule 2 is "Announce a Method." Conflict can be prevented if people have confidence that there is a way and a means for their opinions to be taken seriously. Thus, their self-confidence will be stronger and their ability to function in times of stress will be enhanced. More importantly, they may be able to stick with problem solving instead of becoming so distressed that they go into conflict.

Two types of methods need to be announced and followed explicitly. One is a method for people to express their ideas in good times; when issues are being discussed and problems are being solved. The other is a method that will be used to allow people a hearing in bad times; when the stress is great and feelings are strong.

As you, no doubt, recognize, the difference between good and bad times is the distinction I have been making between stress and distress. People need to know that they will be listened to and that even if, or when, they have crossed the line and are in conflict, leaders will treat them with dignity and provide the means for them to calm down and come back across the line to stress from distress.

For best results, these two types of rules need to be stated, agreed upon, and written down, if at all possible. I can think of no better use of family, committee, board, friendship, or church time than the moments spent in trying to reach agreement on the exact way conflict will be prevented when it arises. Children will be impatient; committee members will feel precious time is being wasted; and congregational members may seem bored; but I guarantee you they will change their minds after the rules have been used to assure them a chance to express themselves or to calm them down when they were in danger of becoming distressed. They will all be thankful that time was taken to prepare relationships for the inevitable.

You will remember the Did section in the "Conflict Requires Analysis and Action" chapter. It was recommended that Helpers, who were going to try to assist in conflict reduction, think back and see if they could decide what had happened. In addition, Helpers were encouraged to reflect on what they could have done to detect, deter, and detain the conflict. Detect and deter are explicit components of what good conflict prevention rules should include.

In regard to detect, each person in the family, committee, board, or church (member and leader alike) should pledge themselves to be vigilant and observant of each other. They should agree to pay attention to the signs of impending distress. They should agree to take each other seriously and not ignore or discount the signs that the stress is becoming hard to handle. Everyone should be willing to stop debate over whatever problem is being discussed and to attend to the feelings that are being aroused. They should commit themselves to lay aside the issue and interact with each other on a feeling basis until everyone is on an even keel again.

Of course, this will not be easy to do. Most of us in a discussion want to press our point of view and win the argument, if at all possible. When we reflect on what has happened in conflict, we will often have to admit that we saw the signs but failed to attend to them. Even when we have been part of groups that had written rules stating that we would not do as we did, we failed. Yet, there will be far more times when the rules are obeyed than would have been true if they had not existed in the first place.

Deterring conflict is yet another matter that requires stated rules to be most effective. When conflict is detected, some explicit ways of keeping it from happening, or deterring it, should be agreed upon. I once heard a leader say to the group, "I want you to know that there may come times in our meeting when I will raise my hand and "stop the music," so to speak. I hope you will trust my leadership at that time. I will try not to do that too often. But if I see one of us going into conflict, I intend to take the position that we are more important than the issues we are discussing. Further, I hope you will agree that we will make better decisions and do better work if we are all out of conflict. What I intend to do is this: State that I perceive the atmosphere is becoming too heated and that we are in danger of going into a distress mode. I will invite us to discuss our feelings. When I do this, I want your pledge that if it is you who are feeling upset, that you will be honest in sharing what you are experiencing. At this point, I would hope we could hear the emotions and reassure each other of our good will. This may sound innocent and naive, but I am convinced it will work. Are you with me?" This was excellent rule setting. The only thing better would have been to write it down and get everyone to sign it.

A well-known illustration of this kind of conflict prevention is the agreement many of us sign when we enter hospitals for treatment. The agreement usually states that, in addition to our agreeing to pay the bill for the services we receive, we also agree that if there is a dispute over the bill we will not go to court but will be willing to submit the bill to a mediator. We further agree that if mediation fails we will agree to have an arbitrator make the decision with which we will abide.

The difference between mediation and arbitration is whether the recommendation is binding or not. In mediation, we agree to meet with a third party who will listen to both sides and try to help us reach an agreement. The mediator may even make a recommendation, but neither of us is bound by it. We may accept it or not. In arbitration, after listening and advising, the arbitrator acts like a judge and takes the issue under advisement. Each party has agreed that they will accept the decision of the arbitrator as final. In both mediation and arbitration, the hospital has tried to prevent the kind of situation in which persons go into conflict and become distressed.

This chapter has dealt with conflict prevention. As I said at the beginning, much conflict can be prevented, although conflict will never disappear. The road to conflict prevention is filled with land mines such as our own fears of criticism, our convictions about right and wrong, our judgments about each other, and the transgressions of those who take freedom as a chance for license. But the guarantee is just as sure: where attention is given to being sensitive to each other and setting rules for how stress and distress will be handled, much conflict can be delayed, if not bypassed completely.

Try your hand on the case that follows. The case is called "Too Liberal for My Blood." It describes a situation in which a long-time church member goes into conflict over the behavior of her new pastor. Although the setting is in church, think of it as an example of what could happen at home, in a committee, on a board, in many types of situations. Ask yourself what you might have done in the pastor's role to have forestalled this situation. What kind of rules might have prevented this conflict?

▼

TOO LIBERAL FOR MY BLOOD

It was about the fourth week that the new pastor, James Green, had been leading worship services at the Parker Memorial Nazarene Church. The only new thing he could remember having done differently was to have visitors stand and identify themselves at the third Sunday service. He had encouraged the congregation to reach out to the visitors and extend a welcome to them by handshakes or hugs or what-ever they felt was appropriate. Thus it came as a surprise to him to be told by one of the ushers that he had better talk with Sister Elizabeth because she was very upset.

It was 9:20. The Sunday service was to begin in ten minutes. Reverend Green had a vague idea who Sister Elizabeth was, so he walked over to where she was sitting and greeted her with a warm "Hello, I'm Reverend Green. You're Sister Elizabeth. How are you doing today?"

"Not very well, Pastor, " she responded. "I would like for you to drop my name from the membership of the church." Her face was red. Her voice was loud.

Reverend Green was taken back by such a request from somebody he had just met. "Why would you want to do such a thing?" he queried.

"I don't want to belong to a church that would lower itself to worship with worldly churches," she responded as if he would know exactly what she meant.

It turned out that she was reacting to a statement in the church bulletin that "Parker Memorial Church will host a union Christmas service on the evening of December 24 for all churches in the vicinity."

She thought this meant an interdenominational service, but it was only intended to mean all other Nazarene churches. She stuck by her request, however, because this was just the last straw in her thinking. She felt that the new pastor was "too liberal for her blood."

Background

Parker Memorial Nazarene Church was an old church that had been the bastion of conservative theology during its heyday. As the neighborhood changed, the membership decreased and the past four pastors had come to Parker Memorial right out of seminary. None of them had stayed longer than three years.

James Green was the latest of the four pastors to come to Parker Memorial. He was eager to try to stop the membership decline and to restore the church to its former grandeur. His encouraging the congregation to welcome the visitors and his inviting other Nazarene churches to join in a Christmas Eve service were part of his effort to enliven the congregation.

Sister Elizabeth was a widow who had been a member of the church for more than fifty years. She remembered when they had over nine hundred persons in Sunday School and more than that number in the worship services. It was distressing to her to see the church lose members. Although many other people credited the decline to members moving away and the changing neighborhood, Sister Elizabeth felt it was due to the loss of fundamental, conservative beliefs on the part of the ministers. She felt that the seminaries were turning out ministers who no longer believed in the old-fashioned gospel and that the only way to turn the church around was for the ministers to return to the faith of the past.

When Reverend Green explained that the invitation to the Christmas Eve service did not mean that Parker Memorial Church was joining with worldly churches but was an invitation to other Nazarene churches, she still was not satisfied. She said, "You are just like all the other young pastors we have had. Pastor Bill desecrated the church grounds by wearing shorts to a work bee. Pastor Henry wore a red watchband. And you desecrated the Lord's House by preaching beside the pulpit instead of behind it. I still want my name taken off the church roll."

Even though the morning service was about to begin, Reverend Green sat down in front of her and said that he was sorry for having offended her. He asked for her forgiveness and held her hand while he talked. There was a moment of silence, then she withdrew her hand. He felt he had not heard the last of the issue.

During the next half hour, Reverend Green noticed that there was a lot of lively conversation going on outside the sanctuary. He noticed that Nicholas, Sister Elizabeth's nephew, was calling people outside and talking fervently with them. As the service started, he noticed that Nicholas was going up and down the aisles grabbing people to go out and talk with him.

Right in the middle of the announcements, the head usher of the church asked if he could make an announcement. He started out quietly. Then his voice began to shake. He began to rebuke all the "Pharisees and hypocrites" in the church. He looked at the people who were leaving with Nicholas and shouted at them. He encouraged all the congregation to support the new minister. When he stopped, there were many "Amens" heard.

Reverend Green, who by now was realizing that he had a major problem on his hand, assured the congregation that the board would look into these issues at its next meeting. He urged those with ideas on the subject to channel them through the board members.

Attendance at the Tuesday night board meeting was high. The discussion was businesslike until it came to the issue of the new pastor's leading of worship. One of the members, who rarely attended board meetings, quoted from the Nazarene books of order and suggested the pastor was violating the sacredness of the service. The pastor did not see the connection between the quotations the board member was using and his behavior. Other of the board members accused the complaining members of being Pharisees. They wanted to disfellowship them for disrupting the Sunday service.

The pastor ruled any motion to disfellowship members out of order and suggested they continue the discussion at a later meeting when their feelings had cooled a bit.

Predicament

Reverend Green did not consider himself a liberal. He did not realize that welcoming visitors and preaching from the side of the pulpit would classify him as liberal in some peoples' eyes.

But he had to admit that something had provoked a serious feeling of distress in Sister Elizabeth, her nephew Nicholas, and several other people. He was "too liberal for their blood."

On the other hand, others in the congregation were offended that this group had disrupted the Sunday service. They disapproved of these people not supporting the new pastor.

The board decided to meet again in one week. *What should I do in the meantime? Maybe I don't have to preach from the side of the pulpit. But that doesn't make me a liberal,* he thought to himself.

What could have been done to prevent these persons from going into conflict?

▼

CHAPTER EIGHT

Self-control: the key to personal conflict prevention

▼

If you can keep your head while those about you are losing
theirs, and blaming it upon you . . . .
— Rudyard Kipling

By contrast, the fruit of the Spirit is love, joy, peace,
patience, kindness, generosity, faithfulness, gentleness,
and self-control.
— Paul (Gal. 5:22)

▼

Rudyard Kipling and Paul said the same thing. The key to *personal conflict prevention* is "self-control," which results from "keeping one's head" while other people are losing theirs. Keeping one's head means controlling the way one thinks. It is our thoughts that dictate our feelings, guide our actions, and determine who we are. It stands to reason that if we want to prevent ourselves from going over the stress/distress line into conflict, we will need to control the tendency to think desperate thoughts. When we think a catastrophe is occurring, we tend to take drastic actions to restore our self-esteem. Keeping our heads in the midst of turmoil is a skill that can be acquired. Loss of control can be prevented.

In the last chapter we considered group conflict prevention. The goal of this chapter is to learn the skills of *personal* conflict prevention. These skills are worthy of the time and effort it will take you to learn and practice them. No one likes hotheads who pop off and become defensive at the slightest provocation. Those who keep calm when storms rage are highly esteemed. The Book of Proverbs speaks of this skill again and again. Note these verses from the New International Version.

▼ "When words are many, sin is not absent, but he who holds his tongue is wise" (Prov. 10:19).

▼ "A gentle answer turns away wrath, but a harsh word stirs up anger" (Prov. 15:1).

▼ "Better a patient man than a warrior, a man who controls his temper than one who takes a city" (Prov. 16:32).

▼ "A fool shows his annoyance at once, but a prudent man overlooks an insult" (Prov. 112:16).

▼ "Like a city whose walls are broken down is a man who lacks self-control" (Prov. 25:28).

▼ "A fool gives full vent to his anger, but a wise man keeps himself under control" (Prov. 29:11).

These are strong words. As an echo to Proverbs, Kipling stated that those who were able to keep their heads while those about them were losing theirs "gained the world." Most importantly, he concluded that such persons would be *real men.* And, we would add, *real women,* too, because self-control is one of the prime ingredients of real personhood.

For Christians, Paul adds a further distinction: those who are self-controlled will be known as those who walk and live by the Spirit of God (Gal. 5:25). A higher honor would be hard to come by. Personal conflict prevention skills are truly worthy to be achieved.

Keep Memory Alive and Well

The first step in personal conflict prevention is to keep memory alive and well. And what "memory" is it that helps keep conflict in check? It is the memory that God loves us (John 3:16). We can rest secure in that truth. Our *identity* is that we are made in His image (Gen. 1:27), and we are put on earth to be His ambassadors (2 Cor. 5:20). Our *status* is that of forgiven sinners (1 John 2:12), who yet are called to high standards (Matt. 5:48). This identity and this status add up to a positive *self-esteem* that is hard to shake.

When that memory of God's love and His expectation is kept fresh and clear, it provides a firm foundation for life. This kind of confidence is like the proverbial house built on a foundation of rock, which Jesus told about in His parable (Matt. 7:24–27). As contrasted with those homeowners whose house foundations are sandy, wise persons who build on rock have houses that withstand rain and flood and wind. When self-esteem is built on the firm foundation of the love of God, seen supremely in Jesus Christ, persons can keep their cool, control their emotions, and withstand major onslaughts. They can forestall the inclination to go into conflict except in the very worst of storms.

When John Wesley, the founder of Methodism, came as a missionary to Georgia, he sailed on the same ship with a group of Moravian Christians from Germany. During the voyage, a severe storm arose and all the passengers came together in the hold of the ship to pray for safety. However, the Moravians stayed on deck and went about their duties singing hymns. When the storm had passed, Wesley asked them how they could stay calm in the midst of the storm. They answered, "Our people are not afraid to die; we rest secure in the love of God; we are in God's hands." They kept memory alive, and it provided security in the midst of the storm. As Isaiah states, God "giveth power to the faint: and to them that have no might he increaseth strength" (40:29). The results of memory for transcendent living are amazing. "They that wait upon the Lord shall renew their strength; they shall mount up with wings as eagles; they shall run, and not be weary; and they shall walk, and not faint" (Isa. 40:31). I am unaware of a better or more beautiful metaphor of the power of memory for self-esteem.

Having agreed that keeping the memory of who one really is alive is a major key to personal conflict prevention, the next question is "How does one do this? How can persons keep their heads? Achieve self control?" This is an excellent question because the memory of God's love for us is not easy to hold onto in the face of everyday life.

Everyday life is similar to "all the forces of nature" that Rachel Carson wrote about in describing volcanic islands that thrust themselves above the surface of the ocean waves with one final blast. She said that these islands build up from the ocean floor through eruption after eruption. When they finally rear their heads above the waves, "all the forces of nature conspire to beat them back down again," according to Carson.

So it is with Christian memory. Everyday experience beats it down in our minds. The memory of God's loving care recedes from our conscious to our subconscious mind. Then, memory tends to almost disappear in the business of day-to-day life. Common experience is based on what we can see, hear, smell, taste, and feel. But rarely does the love of God show itself to our five senses on a moment-by-moment, daily schedule. We have to look hard to find God's love. Often, we come back from our searches empty-handed. Life, like Carson's "forces of nature," forces the memory of God's love back, back, back into the recesses of our minds. We need ways to keep the memory alive, to bring it to the forefront of our minds again. Asking "How do I do it?" is a perfectly reasonable question. I will suggest some steps to follow.

Association

There are many programs available for strengthening our memories. Almost all of them say that a first step is to practice *associating* things with what you want to remember. For example, I shared with a friend a visit I had with my five-year-old grand-daughter. My friend asked, "Which son of yours is her father?" I answered, "Allen." "Oh," he replied, "Allen; that's the middle son who works in computers and went to UCLA. Right?" He was, of course, correct. But, note how he put together all the things he associated with my son to bring the memory back to mind. He had not seen my son in over ten years but remembered him by association!

Remembering God's love and, thus, strengthening our self-esteem requires these same kinds of associations. For example, in my case, reminding myself each morning of the events of my life that I associate with the love of God strengthens my memory and helps me go through the day with higher self-esteem. Such events as the comfort of faith when my father died, joining the church at six years of age, my mother's example of faithfulness, my adolescent decision for Christ, my membership in the Royal Ambassadors, my study of the New Testament—all are things I associate with my "God loves you" memory.

There is an ancient Greek hymn that illustrates this principle of association. It is what is called an antiphonal hymn, in which a question is asked in the first part of the verse and an answer is given in the last. The hymn pictures a young person standing at the foot of a mountain on top of which rests a monastery. The youth is thinking about entering the monastery. He is shouting questions up to the abbot who is standing on the mountaintop. "Will it be worth the climb?" he asks. The abbot answers, "Saints, apostles, prophets, martyrs answer *yes!*" Associating his decision with the testimonies of others cements the youth's decision and he makes the climb. Bringing back into memory experiences surrounding the love of God makes it stronger. You can do this, too. Put the book down and make a mental list of some events in your life that you associate with the memory of God's love for you. Most importantly, intentionally identify several verses from the Bible that state firmly God's love for us. Recall mental pictures of those whom you have known who have been persons of faith. Memorize these and be prepared to refresh your own memory regularly and frequently with these associations.

 Put the book down and follow the instructions.

These Bible verses and events in your life function like associations to strengthen your memory and guarantee that when you face the stresses of life's problems you will be more likely to remember where your true self-esteem lies. As Isaiah 26:3 proclaims, "Thou wilt keep him in perfect peace, whose mind is stayed on thee." This is the promise. It is good religion; it is good psychology. Associating things with our memory of God's love strengthens our recollections and helps us "stay," or "focus," our minds on God in the midst of stress. Thus, going into conflict is less likely.

These associations can be recalled in off-moments such as while riding in an elevator, stopping to wait on a traffic signal to change, listening for a voice while "holding" on the phone, walking to the store, taking a bath, etc. They can also be recalled in on-moments such as when entering a meeting, debating an issue, sharing an opinion, arguing with a loved one, being confronted by a boss, talking after an auto-accident, when making an important decision, asking for a refund, etc. Association works! Memory helps us resist distress.

Time to Think

Another step in strengthening memory is *setting aside time to think*. Many Christians call this their "devotional time." During these moments they read the Bible, study religious writings, think, pray, and commit themselves to listening for God in the midst of the problems they will face that day.

Setting time aside for prayer and study is a first cousin to association, but it is different in that it is usually a set part of the daily schedule. It is not something that is done best on an irregular basis or when one happens to think to do it. It is like physical exercise; it should be done a certain number of times each week.

This method for personal conflict prevention is a way of deepening one's spiritual life. And that is what we want to do, is it not? We want to strengthen the kind of life that is lived out of the spiritual reality of God's love. We want to resist the temptation to think that the only reality is what we experience through the five senses. Our goal is transcendent living.

This does not mean that we spiritualize everything. Problems are real. God gives us tasks to do here and now. It does mean, however:

▼ that we cultivate a perspective;

▼ that we rank things in their true priorities;

▼ that we are able to transcend the petty and the unimportant;

▼ that we gain the skill of discernment; and

▼ that we remain calm when we are threatened.

Our basic prayer should be that we will remember who we are during the stress of the day and that God will be present with us to remind us of His love. There is a much greater likelihood that we will not forget *if* we have set aside this time and intentionally put our mind to thinking about God's love for us.

There is a hymn that most of us have sung that speaks directly to this practice of setting aside time to think. Its title is "Take Time to Be Holy." Some of its words are:

> Take time to be holy, speak oft with thy Lord,
> Abide in Him always, and feed on His word . . .
> Take time to be holy, Be calm in thy soul;
> Each thought and each motive, beneath His control.
> Take time to be holy, the world rushes on,
> Spend much time in secret, with Jesus alone.
> By looking to Jesus, like Him thou shalt be,
> Thy friends in thy conduct, His likeness shall see.

It is important not to think that God will make life smooth for us, or that we will have no problems. This is not possible, nor is it God's will. It wasn't true for Jesus, and it won't be true for us. The cross is a good example of the fact that life cannot be lived without stress. We need the strength and self-control to face reality and not give in to distress or go into conflict.

Giving in to distress is the "evil" that we want to avoid and from which we ask God to deliver us. This is what the Lord's Prayer means. The prayer that Jesus taught us does not ask God to deliver us from the stress of problem solving. It does implore God to deliver us from the temptation to give in to evil reactions to the problems of life.

Taking an Inventory

Turning to some more general, and less specifically religious, skills for personal conflict reduction, there are some time-tested ways to keep our bodies, as well as our minds, from overreacting to stress. First, we need an *inventory of the unique ways our bodies react* when they are under stress. Most importantly, we need to be aware of what we do when we are about to cross over into distress. Bodily reactions to strain and stress are natural; they are normal; they are neither good nor bad; they just are. They are signals to our mind, however, that danger may lurk around the next corner. We can become more conscious of what our bodies are trying to tell us. Many doctors have analyzed this "General Adaptation Syndrome" (G.A.S.). They have noted the increase of blood flow to the brain, the narrowing of the eyes, the faster beating of the heart, and the tensing of the muscles—these are the body's way of preparing us for defending ourselves against threat. The feelings of threat we experience may be heightened by these signals the body sends. If we can recognize when our parasympathetic nervous systems are causing these physical changes to occur, we can possibly exercise some control over them and reverse them. Furthermore, we can control our tendency to catastrophize situations. We can calm our bodies down and think rationally about what is happening.

This kind of control is difficult because these changes happen automatically and unconsciously. Nevertheless, we are learning more and more about how to become aware of what is going on. We are learning how to intercede between the G.A.S. and desperate feelings of danger and threat.

The physical reactions have long been thought to be unmanageable. But control is not impossible, as modern research has demonstrated. If we can keep ourselves from feeling so stressed out in these physical ways, it is likely that we can remain in self-control longer and avoid going into conflict. There are skills for managing the body's stress reactions, and they can be learned.

The body reacts quickly and indiscriminately to the sense of danger. It wakes us up. It is nature's way of keeping us alive. It is the primitive survival instinct operating. The body tends to make every situation into a disaster and act as if every event could be life threatening. However, that is not true. It may have been true in our distant, primitive past, but it is not true today for those of us who know we are secure in God's love. If we can learn to defuse the body, we will gain the time for our minds to make distinctions between those situations which are, and are not, true calamities.

So, the first step is to take an inventory of yourself and identify what physical changes occur when your body thinks there is danger. Not everybody is the same. Do you perspire? Get red in the face? Experience tightening of the stomach? Feel your muscles tense? Feel your bones tighten? Get dry eyes? Have sweaty palms? Become thirsty? Take a moment to do an inventory and see if you can recall these signs of the General Adaptation Syndrome in yourself. Remember, everybody does it. It's not good or bad; it just is.

 Put the book down and follow the instructions.

Do you have a list? Now the problem becomes what to do about these bodily reactions after you have identified them.

Christian Relaxation Exercises

I have written a book called *Relaxation for Christians,* which goes into detail on how to calm the body down. You might want to read it. In the book I suggest that you learn and practice three types of bodily control. They differ in the amount of time they take and the environment in which you can practice them. The first one takes only a few minutes and is called "Quickie." The second type takes about fifteen minutes and is called "Break-time." The third exercise takes about one hour and is called "Deep-muscle." Each of them has a double goal: (1) to help you relax when stress arises, and (2) to help your body learn to be calmer, less tense, and less reactive in the midst of stress.

Quickie

The Quickie exercise is something you can do in a minute. Take a deep breath, then slowly exhale. Repeat this several times. Speak to your body silently. Having identified which part of your body has gotten tense, tell that part of your body to relax. Say to your body, "Loosen up, quiet down, return to normal." As you breathe in and out slowly, say to yourself, "Calm body, quiet mind; calm body, quiet mind."

Then, repeat one or two of your favorite Bible verses, reminding yourself why you can remain calm without getting upset. One verse I have found reassuring is Psalm 118:24 (NRSV), "This is the day that the Lord has made; Let us rejoice and be glad in it." Sometimes I change the "we" in the verse to "I" so that it says, "*I* will rejoice and be glad in it." These verses reconfirm that God loves us; therefore, there is no need to make a catastrophe out of the stress we are facing as we solve the problems of life. God is in control of our lives, and He will stand with us no matter what happens. We do not need to go into conflict and fight for our lives.

The good thing about the Quickie exercise is that you can do it without anyone knowing. You can quiet yourself silently, but intentionally, in a minute or two and gain some control over yourself. Practice the Quickie exercise several times.

 Put the book down and follow the instructions.

Break-Time

The Break-Time exercise takes longer than the Quickie. It cannot be done in public because it will make you appear strange or odd. It requires you to leave the scene for best results. It should take about fifteen minutes, although some effect can be gained in less time.

So, the first step in Break-Time is to take a break. This means that you have to get away from the problem situation. This is more feasible than we often think. Mistakenly, we often assume that we are trapped; that we can't get away from our problems; that the stress situation imprisons us; that we have to stay right there and fight it out. This is not true. We can take a break and then come back refreshed and relaxed.

The very best way to take a break is to ask to be excused because you have to go to the restroom. Humorously, but truthfully, nobody will refuse you the chance to go to the bathroom. Think about it. What parent would keep confronting a child without hesitation if the child said, "Mommy, I need to go to the restroom"? What spouse would hesitate to say, "OK," if, in the midst of an argument, the companion were to say "I'm about to pop; I need to go to the toilet"?

Once in the privacy of a bathroom booth you can practice the Break-Time exercise successfully. The reason that Break-Time requires privacy is that people will think you are odd if they see you close your eyes, grip your fingers into fists, clench your jaw, bend your legs, tighten your stomach, tense your biceps, and scrunch your toes as you take a deep breath and hold it. But you can do this when you are by yourself. As you exhale slowly, relax your muscles. Open your eyes, let your arms hang loose, and loosen your grip. Other people might think you are on medication if you did these things out in public. But that is what the Break-Time exercise includes—and it works. You will immediately feel yourself relaxing and becoming calm.

Try it. Repeat the same phrases you learned in the Quickie exercise. Telling your body to relax and reassure yourself of God's love by repeating Bible verses and remembering past associations. Breathe in and out slowly for a minute or so. Repeat the process several times.

 Put the book down and follow the instructions.

The tensing of the body may sound contradictory to the goal of relaxation. However, this is not so. Tightening up the body accentuates tension and actually forces us into contrasting body tension with body relaxation. Tightening our muscles makes us aware of the difference in the bodily sensations between body states of threat and stress and those of reason and calm. The combination of these actions will give you a sense of euphoria and tranquility. A number of Christian surgeons go through these kinds of Break-Time exercises just before operating. It gives them self-control in the face of what could become very stressful situations. It will do the same for you.

Deep-Muscle

The final exercise is called Deep-Muscle. It will take you between thirty and sixty minutes and should be done at home in a comfortable chair or in your bed. The reason for the bed or comfortable chair is that you will become so relaxed that it may be hard to walk steadily for a few minutes. Besides that, you might just want to stay there for a time after the exercise is over to enjoy the rest and peacefulness of the experience.

This is an exercise that is primarily aimed at training the body to function more calmly than it naturally would. It involves countering the body's natural physical tendency to defend itself whenever it feels the slightest bit of stress. It involves learning to breathe deeply and slowly at the same time that it includes tensing and relaxing each part of the body from the top of the head to the tip of the toes. It is called Deep-Muscle because it takes the time to focus on body tension that lies beneath the surface sensations. It centers attention on the depth of the muscles and inner organs.

Begin by getting very relaxed, closing your eyes, slowing down your breathing, and telling your heart to beat easily, evenly, and strongly. Then repeat Words of Affirmation to yourself. These include your favorite Bible verses and statements directed toward complete release of the tension from the stress of the day. Speak to yourself about settling down into your bed or chair and trusting yourself to a process of deep relaxation. Instruct your body to let go and rest completely in the security of the chair or bed beneath.

Then, while you are relaxed pray Prayers of Release. Let go all the anxiety, worry, threats, and fears of your life. Give them up to God. These include your awareness of the places in your life where you are experiencing difficulty and stress at that moment. Surrender to God concerns about your health, your job, your relationships, your finances, etc.

Give over to God your awareness of your vulnerabilities—those persons and situations where you can easily become distressed. Confess your sinfulness, your tendency to take things personally, your temptation to hate others and feel that they are worthless, etc.

Follow this by releasing all sickness, disease, handicaps, and illness in your body. Admit your worry about your health and surrender it to God. Let the malfunctioning of your body rest in the security of God's care.

This kind of exercise is not the same thing as your devotional time. These prayers are not complete or well-rounded. They are self-centered, in the best sense of that word. They are confined to prayers for one's self; they do not include prayer for others nor do they ask for guidance in daily living. Their sole intent is to relax the body and gain greater control over the way we approach situations we may face when the exercises are over. Most importantly, they are directed toward making the body the "temple of the Holy Spirit" (1 Cor. 6:19, NIV). This means that the goal is to enhance the likelihood that we will do what God intended us to do, namely, live and walk by faith.

Next, pray Prayers of Acceptance. These include receiving from God His blessing on every situation, problem, physical condition, natural temptation, sin, stress, handicap, life situation, tension, problem, etc., that you have released to Him. Let them all be redeemed and healed by God. Give them over; surrender them to God's care. Accept God's restoration and redemption. Let God redeem you from your sin and restore you to health and wholeness.

Now, turn your attention to each and every part of your body. Start with your scalp. Move down your face to your eyes, cheeks, mouth, jaws, and neck (front and back). Stop at each body part, tense it up and let it relax. Feel the difference. Let the relaxation develop. Now, go inside your mouth. Tell your tongue, throat, stomach, and intestines to relax. Experience the sensation of the body simmering down and letting go.

Move to your shoulders, then down each arm, biceps, forearm, wrist, forearm, fingers. Tense up and relax; speak to each part and tell it to let go any tension that is there. You will begin to sense relaxation deep within each of the muscles.

After this focus on your back, then move to your chest. Tell the muscles to let go of their tension and smooth out. Continue to breathe deeply and feel the calmness grow. Let your mind go inside your chest and attend to your lungs and heart. Tell the air ducts to open up, the lungs to receive air and turn it into oxygen. Continue to breathe deeply and slowly. Instruct your arteries to open up and the blood to flow strongly out from the heart. Tell the veins to relax and let the blood return, cleansing the body of impurities.

Come back to the body surface and go down the chest to the stomach to the hips and thighs—in each case telling the body to relax and function normally without tension. Let God restore the wholeness in which you were created. Let God imbue each part of the body with trust and calm. Let God release the body from the pretense that it had to always be "on guard," ready to defend itself against impending disaster. Feel the tranquility deepen and the relaxation develop.

Go down the legs—the knees, shins, ankles, feet, all the way to the tips of the toes. At each location, tense up the muscle, then relax. Note the difference. Tell each muscle to let go of all its unnecessary tension. Continue to breathe deeply, slowly, and evenly.

Pause when you finish with the tips of the toes and enjoy the relaxation, the peacefulness, the calm, and the euphoria of the moment. Let the body "hum." Feel the blood course through the veins and arteries; experience the lungs inhaling and exhaling; imagine all the muscles being restored to their wholeness; experience trust and rest in God's care. Let the body "hum" with a new state of wholeness. Let your mind be completely at ease and worry free as it trusts in God's "unfailing love" (Ps. 13:5, NIV).

Now, as you have gone down the body, return back up the body to the top of the head. The plan is, "Down the muscles, up the bones." It may sound ridiculous to think that the bones need relaxing; but research suggests that much hypertension is due to the fact that the bones become constricted, over rigid, and less movable as the body remains tense for long periods of time. The hypertension that reflects the body's tendency to remain overly long in a state of preparedness for defense results in a rigidity that can be permanent if it is not controlled.

So, it is feasible in Deep-Muscle exercise to attend to each of the bones of the body, telling them to relax and let go of rigidity and stress. Start by focusing on the toes, the feet, the ankles, the shin bones, the knees, the thigh bones, and, finally, the hip bones.

When you get to the tailbone and spinal cord, attend to each of the vertebrae. I recommend beginning with the eight to ten fused vertebrae of the tailbone area, commonly called the coccyx and sacrum vertebrae. Treat them as a group. Then move to the five lumbar vertebrae of the lower back. Treat each of these individually, moving slowly up the back, telling them one by one to relax and be restored. This is followed by the twelve thoracic vertebrae that lead up to the neck. Consider them one at a time. There is no doubt that assuming too much responsibility for one's self-esteem can result in overburdening the back and shoulders. The vertebrae are the center of the nervous system and can, by becoming over-rigid, actually restrict the nerves and complicate the flow of messages from the brain to the other parts of the body.

Stop here, and turn your attention to the twelve pairs of ribs. Repeat instructions to relax each of them one pair at a time. After attending to the ribs, focus on the shoulders, the arms, the elbows, the wrists, and the fingers. Tell each of them, in turn, to let go of all the tension that might be in them.

Finally, return to the neck and take each of the seven vertebrae leading into the skull. Once you have reached the skull, instruct the whole head to relax. Go from back to front, from side to side of the skull and feel the pressure release.

When you finish, just sit or lay there and enjoy the feelings of utter relaxation that sweep across your body. Let the body "hum." Feel the sound of the body as all systems flow easily, freely, and calmly together. Experience the restoration of your mind and body to that state which God intended. Imagine that all systems are functioning as they should, whole and healthy. Send messages up and down the spine, in and out of the brain.

Finish this Deep-Muscle exercise by repeating the Prayers of Affirmation, Release, and Acceptance with which you began. I guarantee that if you do this you will feel deeply, deeply relaxed and at peace. More importantly, your body and spirit will have become calm and relaxed in a manner that you had not previously experienced. Although the prime focus of attention in the Deep-Muscle exercise is on the body, do not forget that this is done within the context of God's loving care. The body is the vehicle through which the spirit and the mind accomplish God's will on earth. Putting our trust in His redemption and restoration is a way of recommitting all that we are back to the one who created us and gave us life. This combination of physical and spiritual reality prepares us for handling the stress of our lives and helps prevent us from going into conflict. It may also help reduce our conflict when we have become distressed.

This Deep-Muscle exercise will take from thirty to sixty minutes. If you are consistent in repeating this process several times a month, you will acquire a manner of living that will help you resist stress and reduce conflict in a powerful manner.

Psychologists make a distinction between *states of mind* and *traits of behavior*. The goals of each of the three physical exercises (Quickie, Break-Time, and Deep-Muscle) is to cultivate a trait that will continue over many days and many stresses. However, even if conflict prevention does not happen quickly, it is possible to induce states of mind that will carry you through the immediate problem and help you resist going into conflict.

I recommend that you put the book down and make a resolution to take the time to try Deep-Muscle relaxation some evening within the next week. Set a time when you will do it.

 Put the book down and follow the instructions.

There is a saying we counselors often repeat that states, "Insight doesn't heal, but there is no healing without insight."

The insights gained in this chapter will not guarantee success in personal conflict prevention. They are no substitute for a dogged commitment to peace and a determination to prevent war. They will provide, however, the skills upon which self-control and "keeping one's head" can become a reality. I would like to hope that you join with me in strongly desiring to make conflict prevention become a personal reality. I think the apostle Paul would be proud if that were so.

▼

CHAPTER NINE

Peace is illusory; peacemaking is not

▼

Blessed are the peacemakers:
for they shall be called the children of God.
— Matthew 5:9

▼

You would expect me to begin this chapter with this verse of Scripture, would you not? Peace*making* had a high priority for Jesus. It is the only promise among the eight Beatitudes where Jesus states that people will be called "children of God."

Blessed people will be comforted, be filled, obtain mercy, even inherit the kingdom of heaven. Only "peacemakers" will be seen as sons of God, close relatives of the Most High. They will resemble God so much that folk will call them God's "children."

This implies that God is in the business of making peace. And this is so. The peace that God gives is mentioned at least sixty-five times in the Bible. It is almost as if God yearns to restore to the earth the peace of the Garden of Eden. Jesus said to His disciples, "Peace I leave with you, my peace I give unto you: not as the world giveth, give I unto you. Let not your heart be troubled, neither let it be afraid" (John 14:27). The early church knew the absolute uniqueness of the peace of God. No more powerful benediction can be found than appears in Philippians 4:7, "The peace of God, which passeth all understanding, shall keep your hearts and minds through Christ Jesus."

So, peacemaking is right at the heart of what God does and what His children should do, too. Like a family of physicians, school teachers, or farmers—like father, like son. Just as surely as a Kennedy will be a politician, so a Christian will be a peacemaker.

Since peacemaking is so much at the center of it all, why is it that peace is so elusive? And it is, you know. Just when one part of the world achieves peace, another war breaks out. Look at what happened when the Cold War ended and the USSR broke up. New disputes broke out; new wars began. And what is true in *international* relations is even more true in *interpersonal* experience. Unfortunately, groups of persons remain at peace only for short periods of time. Controversy seems to be as typical as cooperation. Disputes seem as common as harmony.

Jesus, the ultimate Peacemaker, was, nevertheless, a realist. He implied that there would always be "wars and rumours of wars" (Matt. 24:6). Knowing all things, Jesus knew the human temptation to proclaim "Peace, Peace" (Jer. 6:14) when there was no peace. He also remembered what the psalmist proclaimed (103:14), that God knows "our frame . . . that we are dust."

In other words, humans love war. For humans, war is the "default" condition; peace is an aberration—to put it in computer lingo. As Robert E. Lee stated, "It is well that war is so terrible; else we would become too fond of it." Humans love to fight, and peacemaking is not what we do naturally. Our "frame" is "dusty" and frail and fragile and easily swayed.

In my counseling, I have found that many people become bored and lethargic in life. Getting angry and upset makes them feel alive. They never feel more energized than when they are in a fight. Many people are like the little boy who said to his friend, "I think I'll go out and start myself a war!" If we equate war with sin, then "all have sinned, and come short of the glory of God" (Rom. 3:23). The "glory" of God is peace.

That is why I say that "Peace is illusory; peacemaking is not." We can be peacemakers, even if we do not kid ourselves that the peace we make will last forever. Peace will only last for a time. It's quite likely to eventually fail, colored by defensiveness and denial.

The Christian Conciliation Service, those lawyers who help Christians settle "out of court," often admit that this is so. Realistically, they admit that they have had good success in helping people resolve their differences, but they have had far less success in getting people reconciled to one other. And that is what peace means, trust in each other or "reconciliation." I suspect you know, too, how hard it is to trust someone with whom you have had a major problem. Unfortunately, this side of heaven, it is true that "Peace is illusory; peacemaking is not."

As Christians, this leaves us with a dilemma: If we cannot hope for peace, then why work for it? The answer is that we are called by God to live life at a level higher than the animals regardless of whether or not we are always successful. This is what the Beatitudes are all about. They are glimpses of what life would be like if people truly lived as God wanted them to live. We are to walk by faith (2 Cor. 5:7), believing that what seems impossible is possible through God. And, in fact, what seems impossible will ultimately be probable when Jesus returns and time comes to an end.

No one ever said there would be more than occasional glimpses of the ideal this side of heaven. As Paul said, we "see through a glass, darkly" (1 Cor. 13:12). The peace that God gives is real, and the peacemaking that we undertake is real, also. But it comes and goes; it ebbs and flows. It is here today and gone tomorrow; it is the sign of that which is but is not yet. However, the effort and the goal is worthy of our time and our effort. As the poet Robert Browning said, "Our reach should exceed our grasp, else what's a heaven for?"

In truth, peace is what goes on in heaven, what went on in Eden, and what will happen on earth. Paul spoke of this as the whole creation "groaning" with anticipation of that which is to come (Rom. 8:22–23). He notes how we Christians also groan inwardly because we have seen in Jesus the "first fruits" of the kingdom of God which has broken into our reality.

Note how Isaiah describes God's peaceful kingdom:

> The wolf also shall dwell with the lamb, and the leopard shall lie down with the kid; and the calf and the young lion and the fatling together; and a little child shall lead them.
>
> And the cow and the bear shall feed; their young ones shall lie down together: and the lion shall eat straw like the ox.
>
> And the sucking child shall play on the hole of the asp, and the weaned child shall put his hand on the cockatrice' den.
>
> They shall not hurt nor destroy in all my holy mountain: for the earth shall be full of the knowledge of the Lord, as the waters cover the sea.
>
> — Isaiah 11:6–9

In other words, natural enemies will live in peace with one another. The April 1994 cover of *Hemispheres,* the United Airlines in-flight magazine, carried a pictorial image of this vision. It reproduced the artist Heather Cooper's painting entitled *The Lion and the Lamb*, which shows a grizzly male lion standing at the edge of a pond. His reflection in the water is of a lamb, however, not of himself. Turned upside-down the reverse could be seen. Here the lamb was standing on the edge of the pond and the reflection was that of the lion.

The vision of heaven on earth is where natural enemies do, indeed, live at peace with each other, humans as well as animals. Peace is possible, even if it is not probable, for we human beings who so easily think of each other as enemies, who so easily become self-centered and defend ourselves even to the point of killing each other.

Each of us knows that there is the potential for murder in every one of us, even if we are religious. After reading the story of the Miami teenagers who mauled and killed the man who stopped to help a young girl who had dodged out in front of his car, someone commented, "What happened was horrible, but we know that there is within each of us the possibility of doing the same thing." We are, indeed, natural enemies of each other. But when the earth becomes as full of the knowledge of God as waters that cover the sea, *natural* enemies will become *unnatural* friends.

We know that the peaceful coexistence of natural enemies is possible even if it is not probable. We have seen it in Jesus. We know it in our hearts. As Immanuel Kant, the eighteenth-century Christian philosopher, contended, there is a natural law deep within us that calls us to do more than what comes naturally. He said, "I believe in the moral law within." Frankly, we Christians do not have an option. Paul states peace as a mandate: "If it is possible, so far as it depends on you, live peaceably with all" (Rom. 12:18, NRSV).

Peace is a possibility, and each Christian is individually responsible to make it become a reality. Peace is not an option. Peace is an obligation. Paul concludes his mandate that Christians live peaceably with the admonition, "Do not be overcome by evil, but overcome evil with good" (Rom. 12:21, NRSV).

Now, this is the first time in this book that I have prescribed what you, the reader, ought to do. If you are not a Christian, the statement that peace-keeping is an obligation does not necessarily apply to you. However, if you are a Christian, then you ought to actively try to make peace whenever you can. Peacemaking is part and parcel of what it means to be a Christian.

I like the way Paul puts it: "So far as it depends upon you, live peaceably." In an earlier chapter I quoted the old saying "It takes two to tango." I changed it to read "It takes two to *tangle*." War will not occur unless two people decide to fight. As the ancient philosopher Seneca stated, "A quarrel is quickly settled by one party; there is no battle unless there be two." Deciding *not* to go to war is a decision that can be made by one party or the other. In the movie *Schindler's List*, Schindler says to the German commandant who amuses himself by shooting Jewish prisoners as they walk across the yard, "Power is not the power to shoot prisoners in the back. Power is having the chance to shoot but deciding not to do it; that is power."

In Romans 12, from which Paul's admonition about living peaceably comes, he clearly states that peacemaking involves resisting the temptation to fight. He writes: "Bless those who persecute you; bless and do not curse them . . . Live in harmony with one another; do not be haughty, but associate with the lowly; do not claim to be wiser than you are. Do not repay anyone evil for evil, but take thought for what is noble in the sight of all. . . . Never avenge yourselves, but leave for the wrath of God. . . . No, 'if your enemies are hungry, feed them; if they are thirsty, give them something to drink'. . . . Do not be overcome by evil, but overcome evil with good" (Rom. 12:14–21, NRSV). This is good religion. It is also good psychology. There are several aspects of this Scripture that prove this point. I would like to lift them up in an effort to demonstrate what peacemaking might look like.

First, none of these peacemaking actions comes *naturally*. This needs to be emphasized again and again. These mandates to bless one's enemy, not to be haughty, refuse to repay evil with evil, not avenge oneself, and give food and drink to one's enemies are as *unnatural* as lions and lambs drinking from the same stream at the same time. They are not what we would normally do as human beings.

It is important to recognize this but acknowledge that peacemaking being unnatural is no excuse. Paul assumes that because we were created in God's image and redeemed by the life and death of Jesus Christ we are able to do these things in spite of the fact that they are abnormal, atypical, unnatural, and unusual. We can respond to God's call; we are able to do the impossible because of who we are. As he says in another place, "I can do all things through Him who strengthens me" (Phil. 4:13, NRSV). Peacemaking is "possible" even though it is not natural.

Second, the key to the possibility of peacemaking lies in Paul's advice to Christians: "Let this mind be in you; which was also in Christ Jesus" (Phil. 2:5). This means that the way of thinking about and looking at the world that Jesus exemplified can be the same way that we look and think about the world. This is an amazing but not incomprehensible claim. As I noted earlier in chapter 7 on "Conflicts Can Be Prevented," it is possible to control our "selves" by controlling our "minds." By letting the mind of Christ become our minds, we can do the hard, unnatural thing of making peace—even when it would be so easy to wage war.

This business of Christ's mind becoming our mind is a critical part of faith. It is based on the double nature of Jesus. We believe He was "fully God and fully man," as the Nicene Creed asserts. That is the reason we think of Jesus as our brother. As the theologian Karl Barth said, "Jesus is who we are." We can, because He did! The unlikely becomes possible because of who Christ was and who we are. We can look at the world and live in peace with each other; we can have the mind of Christ. He was our best example. He showed us what we could do and become. The possibilities of human life are fulfilled in Him.

Next, in the beginning of the chapter where Paul urges us to live peaceably with others, he states clearly how the mind of Christ becomes our mind. It happens by a process called *renewal.* Paul states, "Do not be conformed to this world, but be transformed *by the renewing of your minds*, that you may prove what is the will of God, what is good and acceptable and perfect" (Rom. 12:2, emphasis added).

The optimism Paul expresses here is legitimate. Minds can be transformed by the renewal process. "Old dogs can learn new tricks," as my version of the saying goes. Paul does not put an age limit on his conviction that minds can be transformed to the point where persons do, indeed, reflect the will of God. Most psychologists would agree that profound changes can, and do, occur by mind renewal. Paul was ahead of his time. What he said was what we know; people can change by insight, new understanding, altered perception, renewal of their minds. This is a human potential and a divine gift!

One aspect of mind-renewal is to *put things in perspective.* Jesus admonishes His followers to "not worry" (Matt. 6:25–34, NRSV). How can this be when existence poses so many real problems that we must face? The answer is that Christians are not to worry about certain things but be intensely concerned about others.

When Jesus encouraged His followers to "take no thought for your life" (Matt. 6:25), He illustrated what this meant by reference to clothing and food—very basic parts of existence. What He meant was that we should not be consumed with concern for our own survival; there are more important things in life. Verse thirty-three states boldly what we are to do as Christians: "Seek ye first the kingdom of God, and his righteousness." We are to put things in perspective, get our priorities straight.

It is essential that we reflect on how important are the issues of our lives. It is essential that we let go of our pride and ask ourselves how much our self-esteem really depends on whether we win or lose an argument or place first in the influence parade. Even more to the point, mind renewal means getting a new set of priorities; namely, the kingdom of God—His will, His way (Matt. 6:33). This is like changing eyeglasses and seeing the world in a new and different way.

Even in the midst of what might seem to be the most crucial of arguments (such as who is and who is not a "real" Christian), it is possible to stand back and say "How important is it that I be right? Win the argument? Be proven correct?" Is it not possible that many of our arguments which turn into conflicts are determined, to a significant degree, by our need to defend our self-esteems? Could we ask whether every issue is so important that we are willing to go into conflict and lose relationships with those who were once our friends?

Let us move from the *process* of mind renewal to the content of peacemaking. *Love* is the content of peacemaking. Peacemakers are those persons who bless their persecutors, associate with the lowly, are not conceited or haughty, repay good for evil, never avenge themselves, and feed their enemies. They overcome evil by doing good. They do the improbable by acting on the possible. They take it upon themselves to resist the temptation to do what comes naturally. The content of peacemaking is *love*. Christians love their enemies (Luke 6:27); that is what peacemaking is all about.

At the very minimum, loving means acting toward the neighbor as one acts toward oneself. The very essence of the Jewish, and later the Christian, faith is seeing others through the same eyes as one looks at oneself. This means to treasure their lives, forgive their foibles, have concern for their interests, be compassionate when they have needs. This is the core lesson of the parable of the good Samaritan and the lawyer's question to Jesus out of which the parable arose (Luke 10:25–37). This is the foundation of love, its basic premise.

At the maximum, love results in treating one's enemies forgivingly and kindly. This is the essential core of peacemaking, as Paul so graphically noted by stating that love means overcoming evil with good (Rom. 12:21). This is the hard part of love, but it is the very essence of peacemaking. And Christians are called to do this "so far as it depends upon you" (Rom. 12:18, NRSV). Jesus said, "This is my commandment, That ye love one another, as I have loved you" (John 15:12).

The difficulty of love when applied to conflict is threefold. All three problems revolve around the continuum that has love of self at one extreme, love of neighbor in the middle, and love of enemies at the other extreme. Jesus calls us to use ourselves as the standard. We are, in fact, to love others (enemies as well as neighbors) as we love ourselves. That is a tall order. We are to forgive, indulge, encourage, and help neighbors and enemies in a manner synonymous with the way we treat ourselves. Personally, I am confident that I love myself. Moreover, I am also confident that I know what love of my wife and sons means. But I treat others outside that circle of myself and close family differently. I stand judged by Jesus' call to love neighbor and enemy. But I do not deny that this is the core of peacemaking and, as a Christian, I do not have the option of excusing myself from getting up every morning and taking love as my goal for the day.

I conclude with a tender story of a young boy I saw at a Los Angeles Dodgers baseball game. What he did illustrates for me the optimism with which I would like to close this book. The boy looked to be about nine years old. He was well decked out with his Dodgers cap, his blue jacket with "Dodgers" across the back, his first-baseman's glove, and his miniature wood bat. He had a bag of peanuts in his lap that he munched on between batters. But as each player came to bat he would watch intently and cheer the team along when balls were hit. After a player had struck out, I saw him put his bat down quickly, hang his head, and proclaim disgustedly, "I could have hit that ball." Of course the situation was both pitiful and courageous. Here he was, a nine-year-old ready to catch any foul ball that was hit his way. Realistically, he would never be asked to leave his seat and get up to bat as a pinch hitter, much less as a regular part of the team. Yet, he did not hesitate for a moment to project himself into the game as a real player. "I could have hit that ball," he asserted.

So it is with Christian peacemakers. Perhaps they, too, are all decked out with miniature bats looking at the game of life. Perhaps they, too, would be judged piteously ill-equipped to get out on the playing field. But may they, like this admirable little nine-year-old, not let themselves worry for a minute about their situation. May they forge their way onto the playing field of life and proclaim, "I can hit the ball of peacemaking." They, and you, can. I hope to see you at the game!

▼